New Light on Old Songs

KENNETH SLACK

New Light on Old Songs

*Studies in the psalms in the light
of the new translations*

SCM PRESS LTD

334 01097 7

First published 1975
by SCM Press Ltd
56 Bloomsbury Street London WC1

© Kenneth Slack 1975

Printed in Great Britain by
Richard Clay (The Chaucer Press) Ltd
Bungay, Suffolk

Contents

Author's Note

I express threefold gratitude for stimulus to produce what appears in this book.

I would like to thank my church, the City Temple, who encouraged me to share with them the result of this study at a number of points over my happy seven years as their minister. I especially record again my warm gratitude to my secretary, Winifred Weddell, for invaluable help in preparation of the book, an office she has discharged for successive ministers of the church for over thirty years, but also for much friendship.

Again, I am grateful to Anglia Television for allowing me to present some of what I had discovered, in necessarily brief form, to a wide audience. Peter Freeman, Frank Jones and Wendy Smith have made my visits to Norwich a joy across a good number of years.

Yet again, I am grateful to John Bowden for encouraging me to produce my fifth short book for the SCM Press under his editorship. That the Press should want to produce not only works of pure scholarship but books which try to show how the scholars are helping the faith of the wayfaring man suggests real fidelity to its origins.

KENNETH SLACK

Ambleside,
Cumbria

Abbreviations

AV	The Authorized Version of 1611.
Gélineau	*The Psalms: A New Translation* (Collins Fontana) Not by Father Gélineau, but arranged to fit his psalmody.
Jerusalem	*The Jerusalem Bible* (Darton, Longman and Todd)
NEB	*The New English Bible* (Oxford and Cambridge University Presses)
RSV	*The Revised Standard Version* (Nelson)
TEV	*Sing a New Song* – The Psalms in Today's English Version (Collins Fontana)
Eaton	J. H. Eaton, *Psalms* (SCM Press 1967)
Maclaren	Alexander Maclaren, *The Psalms* (Hodder & Stoughton 1893–4)

Introduction

This short book must begin with a confession. I had been ordained for some thirty years before I realized how rich was the resource of the book of psalms to the man called to teach the Christian faith. That is not to say that I had wholly neglected the psalms in my ministry, but the attention I had given them was more sporadic than sustained. The Roman and Anglican priest saying his offices, in which the regular recital of the psalms has so definite a place, must necessarily have his thought impregnated by them. That had not happened to me.

It is true that I was ordained to the Presbyterian ministry and that had an earlier tradition of exclusive use of the psalter in praise: but it was already a dead tradition which had refused in the past to sing 'human' hymns, but only 'the psalms of David'. Moreover, the psalter was used in its uncouth metrical version, and save for a few psalms, such as the noble 'Old Hundredth', the rugged 124th ('Now Israel may say'), and the simply pleasing 23rd, that particular version must be described as an acquired taste.

I suspect, too, that I was critical, in an unexamined way, of the dominance of the psalter either in that older Presbyterian tradition or in the continuing liturgical material of the catholic tradition. Like Isaac Watts, the great adornment of the Congregational tradition in which I was later to minister, I felt that at least they should be christianized. My generation was severely critical of the use of sub-Christian material in praise. The hatred and the cursings were a great problem to us. C. S. Lewis devoted not a little of his *Reflections on the Psalms* to this problem. The passage of time has not abated my conviction that only a portion of the book of psalms can be appropriated for Christian praise with a good conscience. I am encouraged to maintain this conviction by the recent word of as sound an Anglican as Max Warren. In his autobiography *Crowded Canvas* (Hodder 1974) he bluntly writes: 'Only a few of the Psalms, perhaps thirty, can be sung profitably *and* to edification by a congregation today.'

Thus I try to account for my comparative neglect of the psalms. What then has latterly stimulated a far deeper interest? Oddly perhaps, in view of the literary fastidiousness I feel towards the metrical psalter, it has been the coming of the new translations in these last few years that has driven me to deeper study. Of course I do not place them alongside the Authorized Version and Prayer Book version in literary beauty. (It is interesting to note how *two* versions of the psalms have been present in the minds of religious Englishmen for three centuries and more: both 'The Lord is my shepherd: therefore can I lack nothing' and 'The Lord is my shepherd; I shall not want' are wholly familiar.)

I have relied chiefly on three of the new translations. They are *The Jerusalem Bible*, the work of Roman Catholic scholars, *The New English Bible*, which is, of course, the product of a co-operative scholarly enterprise sponsored by the British churches other than Roman Catholic, and Today's English Version, readily available in a paperback called *Sing a New Song*. I have also made occasional use of the Revised Standard Version and of the English version of the psalms produced by Roman Catholic scholars in a form arranged for singing to the psalmody of Joseph Gélineau.

In addition to the light that is shed on these old songs of praise by the work of the new translators, behind which lies a wealth of scholarly advance in many fields as well as a determination to render meaning in words that have impact today, there is all the light that has come from study in the role of the psalter in Hebrew worship. I have made considerable use of three books here. One is a massive work by the German scholar Artur

Weiser, entitled *The Psalms* in the Old Testament Library of the SCM Press (1962). Dr Weiser stands heir to all the pioneering work done most notably by Scandinavian scholars on the relation of the psalter to the cultus, but is not uncritical of what he would judge to be inadequate recognition of the unique character of Hebrew religion.

One other book is much slighter, although for reasons of the series in which it appeared, it was in two volumes. I refer to Cyril S. Rodd, *Psalms 1–72* and *Psalms 73–150*, published in 1963 in the Epworth Preacher's Commentaries series. An admirable achievement in bringing the insights of recent scholarship quite specifically to the needs of the preacher, the book is at once simple and stimulating.

The third modern book I have used is J. H. Eaton's volume on the *Psalms* in the SCM Press's Torch Bible Commentaries, which being published as late as 1967 give insights into the present position of scholarship on the psalms of a very recent kind.

I should add that as well as these recent books I have turned constantly to two older works, W. O. E. Oesterley's *The Psalms* (SPCK 1939, latest edition 1962), and the three-volume expository commentary by Alexander Maclaren published by Hodder and Stoughton as long ago as 1893. No one will turn to Oesterley for sparkling insights, but many matters of detail find elucidation in his book. Again, no one will turn to a book eighty years old to know, say, the latest state of the debate on sacral kingship in ancient Israel, but Maclaren was so superlative a commentator on the religious significance of the psalms, and commanded a style so strong and elegant and cleansed of the turgid tricks of much 'devotional' writing, that to neglect his extensive work on grounds of its age is a needless deprivation. I quote it constantly in the pages that follow.

The purpose of my book is simple. It is to share some of the light that has come to me on the psalms by study of a kind open to anyone who has a will to it. This is not a work of scholarship, as will be plain. It is a work of study, but a study open to many. Since only some twenty psalms are studied here, it is obvious that if the method appeals to the reader he has plenty of material for its exercise. All the equipment needed is three new translations and a commentary or two.

It is perhaps appropriate to record two or three impressions that have been made on me by this study.

One is that the problem that so struck C. S. Lewis, or that at least he felt to be a major problem in the sensitive reader's mind, that is, the hatred and cursing to be found in the psalms, has not loomed large to me. Once you do not pretend that the whole psalter is appropriate Christian praise that problem is much diminished. What has seemed a far greater problem has been the confidence of the psalmist in material prosperity and physical deliverance as the lot of the righteous. The stripping away of the cadences of seventeenth-century prose and the starker setting forth of the conviction in today's more stripped language have seemed sharply to accentuate the problem. It is plain that the man who stands on this side of the cross of Christ cannot share this conviction without its undergoing some considerable transmutation.

Again, and more positively, this study has brought home to me the very valuable way in which the psalms depart from our somewhat genteel notion of how God may be appropriately addressed. Charles Williams wrote somewhere: 'A great curiosity ought to exist concerning divine things. Man was intended to argue with God.' The psalmist does not hesitate so to argue. He does not argue only about divine things in some abstract or theological way. He argues most of all about the ways of God with men, and the particular man who is writing. There is a sheer honesty about the psalms and the dialogue of man with God in them that might, taken seriously, have a very refreshing effect on our notions of what is devotionally appropriate.

Yet again, and most important, I have been struck by the riches that are there in the psalter for our wrestling with religious questions in our generation. Much recent scholarship, as has been suggested, may stress the corporate use of the psalms, and the recognition of this is often very illuminating. But beneath the corporate use there constantly lies an intense personal experience. The intensity has been constantly enhanced for me by reading it in the language of today. It has not been that modern language has demonstrated the dated irrelevance of the material, but rather that the language of today has made the psalmist again and again our contemporary, questioning and agonizing as often we must do.

J. B. Phillips, who, alas, does not seem yet to have put his hand of genius to the psalms, bore testimony that translating the New Testament was like trying to re-wire a house with the current still on, and constantly giving its shocks to show it was alive. Even to study the new translations is to have some such experience. My hope is that not a few readers will try the experiment for themselves.

Songs of Doubt and Disturbance

'As pants the hart for cooling streams, when heated in the chase' – how lyrical, how lovely, especially when set to music in somewhat saccharine fashion by Spohr!

Even in the Authorized Version, 'As the hart panteth after the water brooks', although the strong word 'panteth' is there, suggests by its beauty and rhythm something lovely. But it wasn't something lyrical and lovely that the poet had seen when he chose this picture to illustrate his theme. It was something full of fear and desperation. The female deer (rightly the NEB translates 'As a hind longs for the running streams') is in a dry and desert place. It may be mother to some young. Wild animals, like man, can manage without food for some time. Deprive either of liquid and death comes swiftly.

The poet has seen the hind stretch out its neck upwards with nostrils quivering in a desperate attempt to catch some faint hint of moisture coming on the hardly discernible breath of wind. Its nostrils quiver in a hope born of desperation; the mind of the beast dwells on the thought of sweetly-moving cooling streams; its mouth is open, and its tongue stretched out, and its breast heaves with grim pants.

And what is being illustrated? The NEB gives it as 'With my whole being I thirst for God, the living God.'

Really? It may have been true for the psalmist; it may even have been true for some of the people who later crowded the temple courts and used this song for their hymn–but it is surely a pretty rare phenomenon today. Once recover some of the original power of the illustration, once picture the heaving flanks and craning neck and desperately twitching nostrils of the parched beast, and then say that our thirst for God is like hers, a total matter of life and death, and you may well feel that we are moving in the realm of the unreal. Our spirits may thirst for security, or enjoyment, or status or whatever may be the driving desire of our lives, but few can honestly say that with their whole being they thirst for God, for the living God.

But before we make sharp contrasts between that distant epoch as an age of faith, and today as a day of irreligion and doubt, we may note that what the poet is writing about is *unsatisfied* thirst. Somehow, especially when we hear the opening words sung, we picture quite the opposite. We think of the thirsty animal arriving at the cooling streams. Its thirst almost becomes that thirst that we would like to have before being offered a long, cooling drink, enough of a thirst to whet our enjoyment. It is seen as just a passing thing, almost a necessary prelude to the sheer physical delight of quenching thirst. We talk of working up an appetite, or a thirst, when we are thinking like that. That is not the picture in the mind of the poet. Thirst has become a raging, terrible thing, and there is no suggestion whatever in those early verses that it is something that finds satisfaction.

For this is a song about homesickness as much as anything. Even that word gets softened inside our minds. Homesickness we think of as compounded both of yearning and of the beauty of the love of home. But that is not true for a moment of real homesickness. That is a shattering emotion, a horrible feeling that life has lost both its meaning and its foundation. The genuinely homesick person feels that he has got nothing under his feet, or that inside him there is an echoing and aching hollow. Again we give homesickness a kindlier aspect because we think of it as satisfied–and therefore proving how glorious a thing home is, and how grand that there is implanted in us that yearning for home.

8

> This be the verse you grave for me:
>> Here he lies where he longed to be;
>> Home is the sailor, home from sea,
>> And the hunter home from the hill.

But it is another poet's simple picture that gives us a truer picture of what homesickness is when he just separates the two words and writes of

> . . . the sad heart of Ruth, when, sick for home,
> She stood in tears amid the alien corn.

Even the corn, the same corn as at home, seems alien.

And psalms 42 and 43, which are really one psalm which at some early point in its transmission has become artificially separated, constitute what one version (TEV) calls 'the prayer of a man in exile'. Exile, yes; prayer, maybe. It is written by a man who is exiled in some fashion; that is clear to any attentive reader. It is soaked with the homesick man's tears. But it is doubtful if it can really be called a prayer. In one sense it can scarcely be called a song. It is a conversation in the form of a poem. It is a man's dialogue with himself about faith, and how hard it is to have it.

Now this is much more to our address today than it sounded when we thought of it as declaring that the good man has as great a thirst for God as a parched animal in a desert land. A dialogue between doubt and faith in the life and consciousness of one man can help us.

This dialogue is clear in the refrain that comes three times in the combined two psalms (as we wrongly have them numbered).

'Why art thou cast down, O my soul? and why art thou disquieted within me? Hope thou in God: for I shall yet praise him for the help of his countenance.' So goes the beauty of the old version, but – as so often – the very beauty and familiarity may hide from us what is being said. Take the freshness and simplicity of the Jerusalem Bible version:

> Why so downcast, my soul,
>> why do you sigh within me?

> Put your hope in God: I shall praise him yet,
>   my saviour, my God.

Here is a man who is having a deep conversation with himself. If religion is to have any living reality for a man, he must have this conversation. Much of the time you may be able to stuff doubts away in a corner of the mind, but when things go really wrong you have to face them and bring them into contact with what faith you have and let the dialogue begin.

So seen, the words of this psalmist about his spirit being like the thirst-crazed deer seeking the water-hole is not a great cry of passionate faith but a brutally candid confession of agnosticism.

> Day and night I cry,
>   and tears are my only food;
> all the time my enemies ask me,
>   Where is your God?' (TEV)

They ask, and he cannot answer. There is no sign of God's activity, vindicating good men, advancing the cause of right. Enemies can easily ask, 'Where is your God?' They can ask it as readily today.

It was not even as though his religious memories helped. Quite the contrary. He goes on:

> My heart breaks when I remember the past,
>   when I went with the crowds to the house of God,
> and led them as they walked along,
> a happy crowd, singing and shouting praise to God.

He had had a special place in worship. This psalm is headed that it is one by the sons of Korah—and they had a special function in worship. He had been a leader there. How marvellous it had been. The Jerusalem Bible uses a grand phrase for the Temple, taken from the Greek version of the Old Testament, for the Hebrew is uncertain in its meaning here. It calls the Temple 'the wonderful Tent'. Strictly the Greek would mean 'the tent of the Glorious One'. It was a poet's word that linked the so solid Temple with the simple movable sanctuary that they had had in the desert days, the days of wandering in the wilderness. The act of worship, worship with the crowds that had gone along to the Temple had linked him with all the past of his people. This was where his deepest roots were. And now he is an exile, and his memories of worship are almost bitter.

Every pastor knows this problem. If a husband and wife have been really joined in Christian faith, and found delight in the worship and fellowship of the church, and one of them dies, again and again there is a fearful problem. The very joy that the house of God has represented becomes dangerously near to bitterness. The effort to come back alone to that which has been most deeply shared is one of the most poignant experiences of bereavement. It is indeed at such a point that an interior dialogue has to go on:

> Why so downcast, my soul,
>   why do you sigh within me?
> Put your hope in God; I shall praise him yet,
>   my saviour, my God.

But for all the brave words to his soul, the man has to confess that the things that make him doubt and even at times despair are very strong. Many will remember the noble verse in the old translation: 'Deep calleth unto deep at the noise of thy waterspouts: all thy waves and thy billows are gone over me.' In fact the first phrase has passed into our common language as something of a proverb, 'Deep calleth unto deep'. But what does it mean here?

It seems that in some way – we don't know how – he was held in exile. He may have been a prisoner of war, up in the north, near the range of Mount Hermon where the Jordan rises and begins its headlong plunge down to the Dead Sea. The NEB goes:

> . . . from the Hermons and the springs of Jordan,
>   and from the hill of Mizar,
> deep calls to deep in the roar of thy cataracts,
> and all thy waves, all thy breakers, pass over me.

The fast mountain streams and waterfalls that plunged down from the mountainside, roaring and foaming, found an echo in the man's own experience. Exterior deep called to inner deep. He was like a man caught in a flooding tide, and the waves and billows were going over him and threatened to drown him.

We need perhaps to remember how strong then was the belief that below the surface of life there still ran and surged the waters of chaos from which God had made the firmament. The floods of chaos represented death. It seems that the man had not only to face exile of body and homesickness, but actual physical illness of a grave kind, too. He felt that he might be slipping down into the waters of death; the waves and billows were drowning him, their roar was as real as the waterspouts of Jordan's source.

There comes then a deeply human confusion of faith and doubt. One part of the man cries out,

> The Lord makes his unfailing love shine forth
>   alike by day and night;
> His praise on my lips is a prayer
>   to the God of my life.

He sounds serene in faith. But then a moment later he is crying:

> I will say to God my rock, 'Why hast thou forgotten me?'
> Why must I go like a mourner because my foes oppress me?

And again he hears his enemy mockingly saying, 'Where is your God?'

That is as human as anything could be – that swithering between faith and doubt, between praise and protest.

One thing that it says to us is that there is nothing sinful in our changing moods. We can take seriously the word about the Father in another psalm, 'He knoweth our frame, he remembereth that we are dust.' But, like our psalmist, we must keep the dialogue going, as he does again with his refrain:

> Why so downcast, my soul,
>   why do you sigh within me?

> Put your hope in God: I shall praise him yet,
> my saviour, my God.

This man is facing depression, depression due to being an exile, depression due to being bereft of most that he held most dear, depression due to sickness, yes, and religious depression, too, because enemies, whether outside him or inside him we do not know, are able to ask 'Where is your God?' But he is *facing* it, and he is facing it with a courageous 'Why?' '*Why* so downcast, *why* so depressed?' He is facing it with more than bravery; he is facing it with such tattered rags of trust and faith as he can pull round him. 'Put your hope in God: I shall praise him yet, my saviour, my God.'

This dialogue of a man with his own soul centres upon something of immense importance. It is: how dominant are we to allow our passing emotions to be? Be honest that you have them. It is no use denying that you feel cast down and depressed, that you are in the grip of this or that desperate feeling. Face them, but bring them to the tribunal and judgment of your best self, and let that self ask, '*Why?*' Alexander Maclaren commented on this psalm: 'Emotion varies, but God is the same. The facts on which faith feeds abide while faith fluctuates.'

This psalm does not say anything easily or glibly; time and again the bitter feelings begin to conquer the man, as they can conquer us. But slowly he climbs, and he climbs towards large thoughts of God and a great trust in God for the future:

> O send out thy light and thy truth: let them lead me: let them bring me unto thy holy hill, and to thy tabernacles.
> Then will I go unto the altar of God, unto God my exceeding joy: yea upon the harp will I praise thee, O God my God.

'Light' and 'Truth' are made, as it were, into persons, messengers that God will send to bring his child home. The thought of God's worship had been a melancholy remembrance ('O the happy days of the past before sorrow struck me'): now the thought of it becomes filled with a joyous hope for the future.

He still needs faith. He still has to face the questions of the enemies of faith, 'Where is your God?' But now he has it, because when in that interior dialogue he brought his fears and doubts to the tribunal of the best he knew the final word lay with faith. For the last time he can cry,

> Why so downcast, my soul,
>   why do you sigh within me?
> Put your hope in God: I shall praise him yet,
>   my saviour, my God.

And this time faith has the last word.

2 'God Doesn't Matter'
Psalms 14 and 53

I can remember when quite young being repelled by the statement with which two of the psalms begin–'The fool hath said in his heart "There is no God".' This was just religious arrogance, taking a smart side-swipe at a man who might on the most conscientious and thought-out grounds, and perhaps even with genuine reluctance, have come to the conclusion that there was no God. Were men, I thought, like Bertrand Russell and H. G. Wells to be dismissed in this cavalier fashion? Must religious men condemn in this contemptuous way those who had come to an opposite judgment?

For I grew up in an age, and emphatically we live today in an age, when to be an atheist is to be most intellectually respectable. Indeed, to be anything else is almost intellectually disreputable. Many of the ablest, most powerful and most wide-ranging minds of our time have come to the conclusion that atheism is the only tenable position. How dare we say that just because they have come in total honesty to that conclusion they are to be dismissed as fools?

But when we come really to study what the psalmist says, and what it must have meant when it was written, we can dismiss this problem from our minds. This is not the point that is being made, despite all appearances.

[Two of the psalms begin in this way, and the two psalms are virtually identical. (The original one, psalm 14, uses the old Hebrew name for God, Yahweh, and the other, psalm 53, uses Elohim. This is not a difference to be observed in the English translation, save in the Jerusalem Bible.) In all but a few verbal points they are the same. The book of psalms as it has come down to us is a bringing together of several collections of sacred songs and poetry, and these words had found their way into two of the collections, and so found their way twice into the psalter as we have it. So the striking opening sentence is not a thought of two psalmists, but of one whose poem so commended itself as to have appealed to two collectors.]

What is it then that the psalmist was saying if he was not arrogantly dismissing the convinced atheist as stupid? Today's English Version makes it clear:

> Fools say to themselves,
> 'God doesn't matter!'

Now in a sense this is paraphrase rather than translation, but if the chief purpose of translation is to convey meaning, rather than the most literal provision of the nearest equivalent words to the original in English, then this is superb.

People were not saying in that day, 'God doesn't exist'; what they were saying was 'God doesn't matter'. In that era the thought of an intellectual atheism was almost non-existent. It may have been totally so.

The psalm was written in a period when the Hebrew people were being much more exposed than they had been to Gentile influence. The climate of opinion, thought and judgment was deeply affected. It was no longer the rather closed-in and certainly unique world of Hebrew religion, of the holy and righteous God of Abraham, Isaac and Jacob. But the Gentile world had its gods; the Greeks were, if anything, over-supplied with them. The believing Hebrew might be inclined to say that such gods were nothing and vanity, or that they had no real existence: 'There are no such gods.' But the people who believed in them did not think that, and there is little or no evidence that at that time there were thinkers amongst the Gentiles who just rejected them out of hand. The Hebrews who said, 'There aren't any gods like the ones you believe in', were the reverse of atheists; they believed in the One Holy God, and dismissed all the rest as mere pretenders.

In that ancient world of the psalmist, therefore, you can say that Jew and Gentile alike were theists, believers in God or gods, not atheists who denied divine existence. The psalmist's point was different. It was that many people had become not theoretical but practical atheists.

I can remember a notice not far from where I lived as a boy which said 'Practical Chimney-Sweep'. It conjured powerfully into the mind the thought of his opposite, the wholly theoretical chimney-sweep, pondering profoundly on the austere theory of how chimneys might be swept, and the problems which might be encountered in such an operation. Never would he soil his hands with brushes and soot! But in fact it is the practical that really counts in that sphere – as it is in the sphere of atheism. There may be, I believe that there are, avowed atheists who live for all the world as if they believed that all life was an offering of obedience to a good and loving heavenly Father. And, sadly, there are men of the most orthodox professed faith, who speak much of God, who live as if the law of the jungle were the only guide for human conduct.

It was, therefore, practical atheism that the psalmist had in mind. It was not what went on in a man's mind, but what went on in his life, his behaviour, that was being judged. For how does the psalm go on?

> Fools say to themselves,
>   'God doesn't matter!'
> They are all corrupt,
> they have done terrible things;
> there is no one who does what is right.   (TEV)

These were men whose lives were being lived as if there were no God, no God of righteousness, purity and truth. It would have made no difference whatever to them whether there were a God or no. If they had any belief in God it had no practical effect whatever upon their conduct. It could be put quite starkly, 'God doesn't matter', or for all practical purposes, 'There is no God'.

Now it is this practical atheism, this living in rejection of all that God stands for, which is a far greater peril today than any amount of intellectual denial. Every now and then surveys of varying degrees of value are made of people's beliefs in the modern world and the results are announced. Most of those which I have seen are supposed to be of some comfort to religious people. For their tendency is to say that however empty the churches may be, however much people seem to have rejected organized religion, most people when pushed or probed confess to some sort of belief in God, and certainly most people would like their children still to receive some kind of religious instruction in school.

We should remain obdurately uncomforted. This nebulous residual belief in some sort of a God has no living effect; it does not alter the quality of men's lives. Ours is a world in which we see the effects of a practical atheism. How else are we to account for the fact that as we get more affluent we become more greedy, as we gain greater education the crimes that we used to associate with debased ignorance–like vicious assault and larceny–escalate, as we grow in our powers so we become more terrifyingly inhumane in warfare and in much else? We live as though there were no righteous judge, as though there were no absolute difference between right and wrong, as though each man could make his own rules for the conduct of life. 'There is no God', 'God doesn't matter'. It is a practical atheism that we see.

It is precisely this practical atheism which the psalmist condemns. He is not saying, as we might think, that the man who denies the existence of God is intellectually dim. He is saying that the man who lives unaffected by the existence of God is crassly foolish. It is not a folly of the mind but of the heart and the will.

17

It is striking what the psalmist sees as the eventual experience of those who live like that. He says 'they will become terrified', (TEV) or, as the NEB puts it, they will experience 'dire alarm'. Not a few people today would say that deliverance from the thought of God as the righteous judge has been a liberation from terror, from the 'dire alarm' that can be found in many biographies of the past. For the subjects of those studies it was their very belief in a God who had at least finally to be reckoned with that gave a dimension of fear to their lives. We read of children then who were frightened by evangelical nurses' crude tales of hell-fire and a God of devouringly punitive righteousness. Now, we may feel, man has said 'There is no God', or if there is a God he is not morally concerned with the behaviour of his children like that, and therefore such terror and 'dire alarm' has rolled away like a nightmare when we become thoroughly awake

Has it? At least the old terror was one which had its remedy. We may regret such a portrayal of the character of God, believing that it stressed the wrong things and made its appeal through the wrong emotions, but it was a portrayal that pointed towards acceptance of God's pardon in Christ. It pointed to deliverance from fear, and a way of life–and the power to live it–in which fear need have no place. 'Be of good cheer, I have overcome the world.'

Today the practical atheist faces a more ultimate, a more final fear. Many people are frightened today, frightened not so much for themselves but for the whole of the world. It does not look as though the things in which the humanist put his trust will deliver us. Education was seen as a means of deliverance from the terrors and ills of mankind; now we read of the need for our police to be equipped and educated in the most sophisticated fashion, for crime has become scientific, the calculated ploy of educated men who use the talents developed by trained minds to defraud and exploit the community. New discoveries and the onward march of science were seen as means of deliverance; now thousands of missiles are standing aimed at the heartlands of Russia and Western Europe which could obliterate, 'take out' is the phrase, whole cities and their populations. Deliverance from poverty and the bringing to the ordinary man of riches reserved in the past for the privileged few was going to usher in a golden age for all humanity; heartbreakingly, it has not. New and rather more frightening ills assail us, a growing prevalence of mental disease and disturbance related, it would seem, to a widespread sense of purposelessness and frustration. Our advances tame old ailments only to see new and subtler ones–most often of the human spirit–take their place.

You could paint a very different picture of our age from that Jeremiad. No doubt many people would have painted a very different picture of the age of the psalmist. Superficially then, and superficially now, you could make a far happier and more encouraging analysis. But these things relate to what we experience in many deep places of our thought and feeling. There is something more finally terrifying in such widespread human failure if we believe that there is no God. Then far from abandonment of belief being liberation, it is the cutting of the lifeline. There is no possibility of rescue.

But our psalm is not just contemptuous of the man who is foolish enough to run life as if God does not matter, nor just smugly aware that this is the route to a final terror when man comes to the end of his tether. It is crowned with a passionate yearning:

> How I pray that salvation
> will come to Israel from Zion!

And it is more than a yearning: it is a conviction.

> When the Lord restores his people's fortunes,
> let Jacob rejoice, let Israel be glad!

As you read the earlier part of the psalm you feel that the writer is in danger of such unrelieved gloom, such total condemnation of human failure, as to encourage those who say 'Let's live for the moment and squeeze what pleasure we can out of life–if things are as bad as that.' This is always the danger of prophetic moral horror, of the reaction of a really sensitive man to rampant evil in society. But the psalm is redeemed from that danger by its passionate yearning for God's redeeming action, and its conviction that gladness and happiness lie ahead.

Here is a salutary warning for the Christian church. It is desperately easy for Christians to move towards total despair of our age. If we do that we both cease to be of any use to God, and we slander his grace and purpose. Always our witness must be infused by an eager longing for God's salvation to become credible to men in our day, and founded upon a conviction that God will bring redemption. Unless we do that we shall in our turn be living as if there were no God, no God to save and redeem humanity. We should have become infected by that which we condemn. We should have become practical atheists, and foolish in our turn.

3 A Lovely and Vile Song
Psalm 137

Reflect on the news of the last few years. Almost a hundred passengers in an airliner are plunged to death in a moment because of a bomb placed on board. The greatest of international sporting events, the Olympic Games at Munich, is wrecked by the carefully planned murder of Israeli competitors. In the struggle that created Bangla Desh the attempt is made virtually to annihilate all potential leadership in the breakaway state. Shop assistants are lined up outside an Ulster shop and the selected victim is then deliberately gunned down. Bullets indiscriminately spray a tourist airport leaving men, women and children dying in a flood of blood.

Why select these incidents? The selection is purely casual. A hundred others of the same sort could be found, and pages could be filled with the description of them. Their peculiar vileness, set over against crimes perpetrated for material gain, is that in them patriotism, glory in national tradition and the intensity of love of country have all been prostituted and degraded so that what was the living tissue of men and women expressing personalities that could live and love and work becomes broken and rotting flesh. Vile, vile . . .

Listen:

> If I forget thee, O Jerusalem, let my right hand
>   forget her cunning.
> If I do not remember thee, let my tongue cleave to
>   the roof of my mouth;
> If I prefer not Jerusalem above my chief joy.

Oh, the beauty of it, the heartrending wistfulness of that poignant loyalty! But read on:

> O daughter of Babylon, who art to be destroyed;
>   happy shall he be, that rewardeth thee as thou
>   hast served us.
> Happy shall he be, that taketh and dasheth thy
>   little ones against the stones.

Listen to the last words in the down-to-earth language of a new translation (Jerusalem):

> Destructive Daughter of Babel,
> a blessing on the man who treats you
> as you have treated us,
> a blessing on him who takes and dashes
> your babies against the rock!

'Here endeth the lesson. And may God add his blessing to the reading of his word!' A blessing on . . . ?

It is the same mixture of loveliness and violence, of man's capacity to love his country, to cherish its freedom above his chief joy, including the joy of life itself, mixed up with, no, leading to the vileness of unnecessary suffering and death.

Now before we get all top-lofty and moral in our Christian superiority we must note two things. It is at least doubtful whether this psalm was ever used in the worship of the Temple, and it is quite certain that it was never used in the worship of the synagogue. It is there in the collection that we call the psalter, and is therefore included in holy writ, but it is not—and perhaps more important—*was* not regarded as fit for the praise of God.

We need not regret that it was included, once we recognize its true status. Nor is this only true on literary grounds, that we should be the poorer if we did not have 'By the rivers of Babylon, there we sat down, yea, we wept when we remembered Zion', and would lack one of the most moving cries of the exile that we have, 'How shall we sing the Lord's song in a strange land?', and the great cry of patriotism that has already been quoted. We could have all that by just keeping the first six verses, and excluding from the canon those appalling blessings on those who should wreak their terrible vengeance.

We need not regret that the whole was included, providing that we do not say that this is all the word of God. We may be appalled by the attitude revealed by some commentators who want to regard every word between the covers of the Bible as divinely inspired. One writes of this psalm, it is 'at first poignant, but finally indignant'. 'Indignant', bashing babies' brains out on the pavement? 'Indignant'? The closing mood of that psalm is not indignant; it is as bitterly vengeful as anything can be, seeing the innocent child whose lips have not yet uttered an intelligible word as fit victim for passionate anger and resentment, calling down blessings on the heads of those who batter such to death.

The first question we have to ask is, Why? Why ever should any man, let alone a man who has some sort of belief in God, some deep reverence for him such as is revealed in the indignant (the word is accurate here) refusal to use the songs of Zion as means of entertainment, why should such a man utter this appalling, this grotesquely beastly blessing?

The reason is there in the early part of the psalm, the lovely part. It was written when the exile was over, but Jerusalem still lay in ruins, and in a sense the horror of what Babylon had done in destroying it was more blatant as they eked out some sort of existence amidst the shell of a destroyed city than when they had looked back to it from the plains of Babylon.

The poet does look back to when they were refugees on those plains. Even their physical surroundings brought sadness to them, for they were men who had lived in a little city on a hill, and looked out across deep valleys to craggy uplands. Babylon might have unheard-of splendour in its buildings, its temples, its monuments and hanging gardens, but it was flat and its rivers and canals and never-ending poplars (for that is really what the 'willows' of this psalm are) gave to the exiles a feeling of flat monotony. Nor had any of the associations of Babylon meaning for them; all their memories are around that little city on a hill. They are like Robert Louis Stevenson in his exile in the South Seas who pined for the windswept grey city of Edinburgh and a land of ancestral memories:

> Grey recumbent tombs of the dead in desert places,
>   Standing stones on the vacant wine-red moor,
> Hills of sheep, and the homes of the silent vanquished races,
>   And winds, austere and pure.
>
> Be it granted to me to behold you again in dying,
>   Hills of home! and to hear again the call;
> Hear about the graves of the martyrs the peewees crying,
>   And hear no more at all.

But there is more than separation from home; there is religious bereftness, too. For the Temple was destroyed, and they were excluded from the land of promise. What did this mean for their faith? What did this mean for their future?

Just when they were trying to face all that, sitting by the river – often in the east a place of worship, as the Acts of the Apostles reveals – and singing laments to their harps or lyres, some of the very race that had smashed Jerusalem to pieces and savaged its inhabitants, and ripped the rest away from home and the securities of faith, come along and cry, 'Come on, sing *us* some of those famous songs of Zion, of Jerusalem' (the very city that they had razed to the ground). What, sing the songs of Zion *to them*–sing *now* 'There is a river the streams whereof make glad the city of God, the holy habitation of the Most High', here as they sit, beside the river of a victorious Babylon? Sing now 'Within her citadels God has shown himself a sure defence' when the citadels are no more, and men are wondering whether God cares at all? Sing, 'His abode has been established in Salem, his dwelling place in Zion', or 'On the holy mount stands the city he founded' when it stands no more?

How, how, God, can we sing your songs, songs like that, when we are in a foreign country and Jerusalem is no more? So they hang their harps on the willows and refuse to sing, to sing of what they had rejoiced in, and which is now no more, and to sing to those who had wantonly and by brute force destroyed the things that the exiles loved.

To all that the singer looks back. And when he looks out now at the time that he is writing the pathos is no less, of a ravaged Jerusalem and a ruined Temple. It is wonderful, very wonderful the faith and love that rise to the cry:

> May I never be able to play the harp again,
>   if I forget you, Jerusalem!
> May I never be able to sing again,
>   if I do not remember you,
>   if I do not think of you as my greatest joy!   (TEV)

It is faith and love going out to a ruin—a ruin that symbolizes all that is dearest and all that is of hope in the future.

There is loveliness in all that. There is glory in it. It is these things that make men truly human, the poignancy of memories, the loyalty even to that which has been destroyed, the refusal to degrade what is sacred to ingratiate yourself with those who have power over you, the hope against all appearances and probabilities, the clinging of faith to God's great promises even when the symbol of them is a sad ruin. There is loveliness in all that.

But it is all that which leads to the vile horror that follows . . . not only in fact against Babylon, but Edom, too. Edom was the little nation just to the south. They were blood brothers to the men of Judah, but in the terrible hour when Babylon was wreaking destruction on Jerusalem they had yapped like a jackal at a lion's heels crying, 'Tear it down to the ground!' 'Remember, Lord, what the Edomites did, the day Jerusalem was captured, remember how they kept saying, "Tear it down to the ground".' And then, 'Babylon, you will be destroyed! Happy is the man who pays you back for what you have done to us – who takes your babies, and smashes them on a rock!'

It is the very passionate feeling which drives this love and loyalty which leaps out of control to rejoice in the thought of this foul vengeance. This is the magnitude of the problem that we see in our world today. Men who feel little, men who are indifferent to their country, to the past, to high and great memories, do not face this danger. It looks as though this danger is there just because men's hearts and minds can be possessed by great loyalties. The more 'feeling', the more passionate a man is, the graver the danger.

Have we just got to swallow this bitter draught, that man being what he is, his very capacity for high and intense feeling for the good and great things that matter is bound to betray him into vileness, and horror and delight in cruelty?

No, but we have to recognize that the danger is there and strive most manfully, and seek God's grace to help us against the descent into this vileness and horror. Guard and examine carefully all patriotic feeling; of all feelings it is most easily exploited to justify what all human beings unaffected by that feeling would readily condemn. What the Nazis did in the Third Reich, what they did to the Jews, and to displaced persons from other nations, would have been impossible but for the malign power of patriotic and national feeling wilfully exploited. Watch, watch like a moral hawk, what is done in the name of nationalism and patriotism. There is a wonderful place for joy in your own country. 'O Jerusalem, Jerusalem,' lamented Jesus, like a lover, which he was. But he was clear-eyed about Jerusalem and its moral failure. Let us beware of the things that are done in the name of patriotism. This psalm, not of deliberate intent, warns us of this.

But the psalm unconsciously teaches that if patriotism is a

grave danger here, religion is even graver. Let patriotism be harnessed to wrong ends and it is terrible. Let religion be harnessed to wrong ends, and let religious feeling get out of the control of morality, and it is unspeakably viler. That is what happens in the psalm. Because Edom and Babylon have not only destroyed the city and wasted the territory, but ruined the Temple and desecrated the land of promise nothing can be too terrible for them. Let the babies have their brains knocked out, for in that way we can be sure there will be no more Babylonians. They will have bred in vain. (It is the same cry as the not uncommon war-time one that all Germans should be castrated, then there will be no further generation to lay Europe waste again.)

Hatred and revenge are given a religious justification, even a religious sanctification. C. S. Lewis comments on this psalm, 'Of all bad men religious bad men are the worst.' 'Beware,' said Gladstone, 'lest you make your religion a substitute for your morality.' Beware of a religion that sanctifies your worst impulses, whether it be to justify revenge, or more genteelly, but as damnably in its own sphere, to sanctify your spiritual pride by condemning the moral failures of other people.

But there is a third comment to be made that runs the other way. Beware of avoiding the temptation towards such vileness and cruelty by becoming merely indifferent to right and wrong. The psalmist was wrong, utterly wrong in his lust to see Babylon's babies destroyed, but the man who felt no horror either for what Babylon had done to the peoples it had subjugated would be not better, but worse. To be indifferent to cruelty, not to have to overcome the temptation to revenge because *you* are all right, is no moral position. In fact the indifferent people drive the others to their excesses; if the world passes by atrocities which have been done, and does not care, the passionate man cries that he must do the outrageous thing just to show that the intolerable has been committed. We have seen not a little of that in recent years.

The final and by far the most important thing which has to be said is that only if true religion has a word to say and a power to wield is there any hope for mankind. For atrocity breeds atrocity. We have seen it throughout this century. Let the realists loose and you cannot have any hopes for mankind. Only if there is in true faith a word which can sever this grim nexus, this endless action and reaction of atrocity and revenge, revenge and atrocity, can we have hope.

So look at a word that was spoken at a different level from that of the psalmist, but at the very time that Babylon had razed Jerusalem and its leading citizens were taken away captive. It is God's prophet Jeremiah speaking: 'Seek the welfare of the city where I have sent you into exile, and pray to the Lord on its behalf.' And these were announced as God's words, God's words when Jerusalem's ruins lay still smoking, when the heaps of the dead had only just been interred.

The contrast is almost incredible. One cries for the babies to be battered to death, the other for a deliberate seeking of the welfare of Babylon. One asks how the Lord's song can be sung in a strange land, the other says that if you cannot sing you can work and pray for the city that has done you vile harm. This word of Jeremiah points to the word of Jesus, 'Pray for them which despitefully use you.'

Psalm 137 is the psalm of the natural man in his glory and his shame. We can be glad that it is in the psalter not to sing it in God's praise, which would be blasphemy, but because it brackets so unforgettably the glory of man's love for and loyalty to his land and people, and the shame with which he blackens it with the lust for revenge. We can, if we like, just use the first six verses, but then we shall not face the challenge of it, which is that both emotions gripped the same man, and gripped him at the same time because they were related to one another.

This psalm does not reveal God, it reveals what is in the heart of man. It is elsewhere in scripture that we have to look for answers to the question this psalm and our present-day world pose to us.

4   If Chaos Should Come Again
Psalm 24

Many feel today as if human life in any really civilized sense were only being lived out on some thin and fragile crust which might at any moment give way and everything be plunged into a maelstrom of chaos and darkness.

Probably few men felt this as much in the last century. Vile things happened then, but they felt that this was just a phase from which mankind was emerging as education and enlightenment did their triumphant work. Today it is different. We feel as if we have no solid ground beneath our feet. We turn on our television sets and see the burned-out remains of villages with the legs of what had been fellow human beings protruding from the wreckage. We see students setting fire to the buildings that were to be the scene of their education and enlightenment. We see other students being shot down on their campuses. The assassin's bullet, the fratricidal civil war, the screams of hatred emerging from radio sets as national propaganda whips up populaces, these are commonplace. How thin the crust of civilized life seems! Bonhoeffer spoke truth when he wondered whether any generation had ever had less ground beneath its feet.

The understanding that the Hebrew people–like many others in the Near East–had of the world they lived in was just such a picture. Learning passages of scripture off by heart is very out of fashion today (and whatever the gains of new translations they certainly do not help us to remember texts). But not very long ago anyone's religious education would have been thought to be very neglected that had not taught him to recite the Ten Commandments. But what did we really make of the last phrase of this part of the second Commandment, 'Thou shalt not make unto thee any graven image, or any likeness of any thing that is in the heaven above, or that is in the earth beneath, or that is in the water under the earth'? We probably thought that it just meant heaven, earth and sea, but the plural in the NEB makes the picture clearer: 'You shall not make a carved image for yourself nor the likeness of anything in the heavens above, or on the earth below, or in the waters under the earth.' Beneath this earth there swirl the dark waters of chaos, those waters above which the Creator created the vault of heaven, and from which he made the dry land to appear, as the story of Genesis goes. Earth and heaven are now here, but beneath them the waters of chaos are still there. It is God's creative word and power that alone holds them back and enables life to go on.

It was with this picture in their minds that men sang the first verses of this 24th psalm. The first verses are a kind of introit; they give us the great wide setting within which we are to see all that follows. The psalm was probably sung at a great festival when the Ark of God was carried into the city in procession.

> The earth is the Lord's and all that is in it,
>   the world and those who dwell therein.
> For it was he who founded it upon the seas
>   and planted it firm upon the waters beneath. (NEB)

The new translation makes far clearer the image that was in the mind of the psalmist. It is the actual picture of the great creation story of Genesis, of the power of God to found the earth and plant it firm even though the waters of darkness and chaos surge below it still.

What they sang had immense force for them when they had that kind of picture of the universe. They literally believed that the dark waters were swirling just beneath them; it was only the wonderful creating power of God that saved them from being engulfed. And it was to that wonderful creating power of God that they offered their praises as they made their way with the Ark to the Temple. In one way they believed that God in some special fashion was related to the wooden box, yet in another way their minds and imaginations swept out across the whole of the world that they knew. They cried out their large creed, that the whole earth was God's and everything in it, and that none of it could exist for a moment were it not that his power held back the black engulfing waters of confusion and chaos from rising.

That is not, and could not be, our literal picture of the physical universe. But the psalmist's picture of God preserving us from chaos and destruction comes together with the sense that television and newspaper have brought of the paper-thin crust that seems to be all that is beneath our feet as we strive to preserve or achieve civilized life today. We cannot have the psalmist's picture of his world: we desperately need his sense that only as men acknowledge that the earth is one, and all men in it, *because God made it all*, shall we find a world that is planted firm and unshakeable over all that would engulf our human life.

It was not, of course, only a sense of God's colossal power that possessed the psalmist's mind, or we should not have the remarkable dialogue which follows the spacious introit that looks out across the world. The procession has now arrived at the gates of the city. The introit has reminded them of the nature of the God whom they seek to worship. They are overwhelmed with a sense of awe and wonder; and they cry out asking who is worthy to go up to the place of worship of such a God.

> Who may go up the mountain of the Lord
> And who may stand in his holy place?

It is one of the great issues of all religion. What does God want of you, what are his demands? And the priest of God within answers the men who are still outside the gate.

> He who has clean hands and a pure heart,
> who has not set his mind on falsehood,
>   and has not committed perjury.
> He shall receive a blessing from the Lord,
>   and justice from God his saviour.

This is an answer given in the distant past. There is not a word in it about being Jewish, that to approach God you have to belong to his special people. There is not the slightest undertone of nationalism. Nor is there a suggestion of the right ceremonial, that God must be approached with this or that formula or ritual, with some particular sacrifice in hand.

The whole answer has to do with a man's inner and moral nature. The Christian faith has a necessary further word to say about the clean hands and pure heart; for no man could stand in God's holy place if he had to achieve these for himself. But the thing that comes home from the NEB is the blazing insistence upon *truth* as the essential condition for a man's approach to God.

The AV does not make this as clear. It reads: ' . . . who hath not lifted up his soul unto vanity, nor sworn deceitfully'. The NEB goes:

> who has not set his mind on falsehood
> and has not committed perjury.

The last phrase may startle us. Why suddenly bring up perjury, of all things? To swear deceitfully is more general: doesn't the NEB make it almost absurdly particular?

On this two things can be said. In the East perjury is almost a profession. When I was in India I went to stay with a missionary friend. We walked around the village, and I was introduced to various notabilities. As we were coming away my friend waved across the road and greeted a man in friendly fashion. The greeting was returned, but the man did not come over, despite the rarity of a new white face in those parts. 'That's our professional false witness,' said my friend to me quite naturally. People paid him to go to the courts and say what they wanted him to say. It was almost a learned profession, like being a solicitor. This was a strong temptation in the East, and required a strong warning.

The second thing is more important. Why does our own system of justice treat perjury as a most heinous offence to be dealt with by most severe penalties? Because it is destructive of justice; once let perjury become common, be treated lightly, and it becomes virtually impossible to administer justice at all. Judge and jury are 'all at sea'. Note that way we have of expressing it, 'all at sea'. It links on to that picture with which we began; the solid ground has gone from under our feet, the ancient waters of chaos begin to rise.

Perjury does that in a public system of justice, and falsehood does the same inside any man's life. If he sets his mind on falsehood – to use the NEB's phrase – he is blocking his way to God's holy place, because once truth doesn't matter, once its reality is denied a man cannot begin to centre his life on the right things, for he becomes too confused to know what they are.

Many parents, easy-going in most respects, feel they have to come down like a ton of bricks on the beginning of lying in a child. Other acts of wrong-doing may seem far worse in their immediate effects; if a child is destructive, for example. But the wise parent sees that for a growing mind to become set on falsehood is far more destructive. It destroys the very basis of a trusting relationship between persons. With a liar you are always 'all at sea'; chaos is come again. A mind set on falsehood is a mind set on self-destruction. Such a mind is incapable of right relationship to God or men. Jesus echoed the dominant thought of this part of our psalm when he said that God is spirit and they that worship him must worship him in spirit and in *truth*. Truth is one of the great pillars on which true human life is founded. Once abandon it and the civilized world begins to sink under the chaotic waters again.

It is this that has given the totalitarianisms of the twentieth century a great deal of their vileness and horror. They have not cared about truth, but only about the propaganda of their ideologies. If a lie served the interests of Hitler or Stalin a lie it was. It was just after the First World War that the poet Yeats with a seer's vision saw what was coming upon us . . .

> Things fall apart; the centre cannot hold;
> Mere anarchy is loosed upon the world,
> The blood-dimmed tide is loosed, and everywhere
> The ceremony of innocence is drowned;
> The best lack all conviction, while the worst
> Are full of passionate intensity.
> Surely some revelation is at hand . . .

The poem closes . . .

> And what rough beast, its hour come round at last,
> Slouches towards Bethlehem to be born.

The daring, almost blasphemous, idea of the poet brings home to us with startling force the degree to which falsehood has invaded the cradle of truth.

It is truth which is the key to the holy place of God. Our truth, our commitment to truth, will only be partial, but what really matters is that we have not set our mind on falsehood, that we know and honour truth when we see it.

But the climax of the psalm is not the entry of man into the holy place but the entry of God. Perhaps this part of the psalm goes back to the bringing of the Ark to Jerusalem by David, the entry of God (as it would be popularly pictured) to that little town set on a hill. That moment was in fact to lead to the old citadel of the Jebusites being a holy city to three world faiths, Judaism, Christianity and Islam. At that first entry it was all thought of rather crudely – the God who had given them tribal, military victory, 'the Lord mighty in battle'. But all this had become caught up into far larger, and more wonderful thoughts of the glory of God's coming to men.

That was true even when they sang that psalm at Jerusalem in later centuries. When the keepers of the gate cried, 'Who is the king of glory?', when the demand was made for the gates to be thrown wide open, the reply came 'The Lord'. Here for full light we can turn to the Jerusalem Bible. Here that translation's use of 'Yahweh' helps. 'Who is the King of glory?' cry the keepers of the gate, and the answer really is 'Yahweh'. Not simply 'the Lord', that is, God, but the God whose name they knew, the God who had told them his name, who had revealed himself to them. It is to that mighty and particular password that the ancient gates are lifted up, and the King of glory enters in.

For study the word 'Yahweh' helps: for Christian devotion we may be glad that the other translations use 'the Lord', for we have another name by which to interpret that word, the name

Jesus. This psalm has claimed a particular place in Christian praise, for example, in the liturgy of the Church of Scotland. It is often sung in its metrical form for what is called the Great Entry at the communion service. The elders go out and return bearing the bread and wine as this is sung. The swelling psalm speaks of the coming of the King of glory to his people in the form of the communion.

Again, this psalm has had a special association with the feast of the Ascension. It has not seemed wrong to sing of Jesus

> The LORD strong and mighty,
> the LORD mighty in battle

for it has been another conflict and another kind of victory that Christian men have thus remembered.

The way in which the Ascension is described in the New Testament belongs as much to an out-dated and untenable picture of the physical universe as does the notion of the earth being founded on the waters of chaos. But equally what is represented remains true, and the truth underlying the two pictures is closely related. Where are we to put our confidence, where find ground under our feet, when the waters of chaos seem to be rising? The psalm tells us, and the gospel deepens its meaning. We put our confidence in the entry of the known and victorious King of glory.

5   God and the Men of Blood
Psalm 139

The book of psalms has a lamentable way of letting us down. You notice it in the 139th psalm, one of the most glorious in the whole collection. For much of its course you are moving in the realm of soaring imagination and glowing poetry. You fly to the point of sunrise or westward across the sea, climbing the heavens, going down to the darkness of Sheol (the abode of shades which the Hebrews thought lay beneath this earth). It is the greatest poem in all scripture about how God confronts us in every experience of life, how he knows us even in the most secret places of our being and motivation, and how he has made us from the moment that we began to be fashioned in our mother's womb. Then suddenly comes the terrible let-down:

> God, if only you would kill the wicked!
> Men of blood, away from me! . . .
>
> Yahweh, do I not hate those who hate you,
> and loathe those who defy you?
> I hate them with a total hatred,
> I regard them as my own enemies. (Jerusalem)

What an appalling intrusion into Christian worship! Even what a spoiling of the psalmist's original work! How bitterly we must regret that he wrecked the whole tone of what he was saying, even singing, breaking off his majestic flight Godwards to drop like a stone into this seething pit of hatred and anger.

It is almost a classic instance of how the indiscriminate use of psalms in Christian worship produces grotesque and even laughable results. But let us be careful not to move from that to such a moral tidying up of the psalms that we make them not the strong meat that they are, but some sort of bland pap out of which all the roughage and difficulties have been taken, leaving poor nourishment for people living in this crude and cruel world. It is at least doubtful whether this kind of thing *was* a momentary lapse on the psalmist's part. At least one scholar writing on this psalm maintains that the real nub and kernel of it is these 'hating' verses which petition God for the destruction of the wicked. It was to make this prayer that the psalmist wrote his poem.

Possibly that may be pitching it too far the other way, but certainly the psalmist who gloried in the wonder of the God who confronted him in every experience that life could hold, who was still with him though light became night about him, and whose thoughts were so wonderful that they were as beyond counting as the grains of sand on the sea-shore, was, just because of that realization of God, totally baffled by the infamy and vileness of really wicked men.

Do we think this is all very remote from us and our lives? How do we react in these days when we read of a father in Belfast carrying a wantonly shot young son down the road pleading for someone to take them to hospital, and no one responds? What are our emotions when we see on television the bullet-spattered walls of some humble living-room in which a man has been killed in front of his wife and children? Isn't there something in us that then cries out:

> God, if only you would kill the wicked!
> Men of blood away from me! . . . ?

Aren't the creatures who do these things the enemies of God, the sworn enemies of the God of love? Can it be wrong to cry

> I hate them with a total hatred,
> I regard them as my own enemies . . . ?

We must be grateful for the psalms as strong meat to chew on, even if sometimes we have to say that this or that passage is really gristle, and have to spit it out because there is no sustenance in it. We do not need for our religion today material that has been made so bland that it cannot really sustain us in this rough world. One thing about the psalms is that they never depart for long from the reality of human feelings, the hatreds, the fears, the questioning, the anguish that add up to the problems that faith has to face.

You may say, 'What place have these things in religious writing? Shouldn't the writer who has exposed his mind and heart to God be purged of these things?' There is something in that; but two things can be said on the other side. One is that if all that *is* kept out of worship then there is a real danger of a divorce between what we feel in the world outside and what we think it to be appropriate to feel in worship. Such a divorce between life and religion is perilous. The other thing is that in a real sense it is just because the psalmist knows God in his wonder and beauty that the problem of the appallingly wicked bothers him so much. Wickedness on a vile scale may be disturbing and hateful to the man without religion, but to the believer in a good and caring God, and a God who has made all things and keeps them in being by his life and power, such rampant evil is a gnawing and terrible problem.

In fact the problem is so obvious that it seems odd to the psalmist that such an all-knowing God, confronting man in every experience of life, has not done something about it. As C. S. Lewis puts it with a characteristically penetrating humour, 'Naively, even childishly, in the middle of a hymn of praise (he) throws in, "Wilt thou not slay the wicked, O God?"–as if it were surprising that such a simple remedy for human ills had not occurred to the Almighty!'

But this is an age-old and genuine human emotion. How many people have cried out down the ages, 'It's a wonder that God doesn't strike him down', when appalled by some more than usually vile act? Underlying such a naive cry there are elements of vital religion. One is that God does care about the difference between good and evil; he is not morally indifferent. Another is that God is not powerless; he is seen as active in the world. Surely if both these things are true then it is reasonable to expect that God will do something about it.

Let us look back to the understanding of God that is shown in the poem until this point that at first seems such a let-down. There are three big things being said about God. Rather they are being said *to* God. How much poorer would be this poem if this were a series of descriptions of what God is like, instead of what it is, the spirit of a man crying out to the God who made him. This very fact says almost as much as the words themselves; it says that a man may speak to this God and be heard. There is what Martin Buber called an 'I–Thou' relationship between a man and his God. He can cry

> Lord, thou hast examined me and knowest me.
> Thou knowest all, whether I sit down or rise up.

It is to a God like that that you can cry out with your problems, to whom you can, in effect, say, 'Look, Lord, at the damage those awful folk are doing to people's life and happiness, yes, to *my* life and happiness; surely you're going to do something about *that*? You can't let *that* go on.'

The God who is so intimately addressed by the psalmist is seen and experienced in three ways. There are three very long and high-sounding words to describe those three ways in which God confronts us. They are that God is experienced as omniscient, omnipresent and omnifacient, but the psalmist puts these things with the concreteness of a true poet, using pictures instead of big, abstract words. So the psalmist does not talk of God's omni-science, he says:

> there is not a word on my tongue
> but thou, Lord, knowest them all

and–lovely thought this–'Thou hast traced my journey and my resting places'–just like a father and mother would try with an atlas to trace the voyaging of an adventurous son or daughter. It is not that God knows everything, in some general and abstract fashion, but he knows me, knowing my thoughts from afar.

In the same way it is not just that God is present everywhere, but he is present everywhere to me. The most glorious poetry in this psalm is found in that picture of the writer trying to flee from the presence of God, climbing to heaven and going down to hell. It is worth noting that this singer of Israel firmly contradicts others of his company–the writer of psalm 6 addresses God and says, 'None talk of thee among the dead; who praises thee in Sheol?', and the writer of another psalm, 88, says

> Dost thou work wonders for the dead?
> Shall their company rise up and praise thee?
> Will they speak of thy faithful love in the grave,
>   of thy sure help in the place of Destruction?

But our psalmist firmly refutes the idea that God is not to be found even in the place of shades. God is everywhere–even there. Even though he takes what the old version mysteriously, but beautifully, calls 'the wings of the morning' and the newer versions call tellingly 'flight to the frontiers of the morning' or 'the point of sunrise', God is still there. In fact if you look at the newer versions, like the NEB and Jerusalem, you will find that while there is a loss of verbal poetry there is a wonderful gain in meaning. There is nothing as lovely as

> If I take the wings of the morning, and dwell in
> the uttermost parts of the sea . . .

but when Jerusalem says:

> If I flew to the point of sunrise
> or westward across the sea

and you link it to what has gone immediately before—the flight upwards to heaven and down to Sheol—you realize the full character of the poet's thought. Go as high as you can, go as deep as you can, fly as far east as the sunrise, or westwards to the limit of the sea—and God is still there. There is no experience of life in which he does not confront you. He confronts you in the heavenly experiences, and the times that you call 'sheer hell', in the freshness of new experiences, those that are like the dawn, and the time of life when the sun is setting in the west. In all of them God finds you, confronts you with his challenges and disturbances and his strength and peace.

Nor is it just that God has made everything, that in the technical phrase, he is omnifacient; it is that he has made me. And how graphic again is the picture:

> You know me through and through,
> from having watched my bones take shape
> when I was being formed in secret,
> knitted together in the limbo of the womb.

It is a God like that that the psalmist knows, a God who knows him through and through, a God who is found in every experience of life, a God whose concern for him 'reached back to the mystery of his ultimate origin' (Eaton). Is it not reasonable for a man who knows God like that to cry out against the wicked? If God were remote, basically unconcerned with the world that he had wound up and left ticking, there would be misery in the evil, but no problem arising from it. It is the very fact that the psalmist knows that God is confronting us in every experience of life, and has been from the moment that he first began to be formed in the womb, that makes God's inaction in regard to peculiarly vile men hard to understand. That sudden cry is not a let-down: it is a consequence. If you, my God, are like that— why, why don't you deal with the wicked, with those called 'the men of blood'?

Sometimes those verses are missed out in public reading, and perhaps they have to be when there is no opportunity for commenting on them. But if we miss them out do we really get the full force of the moving verses that follow and bring this wonderful poem to its close?

> Examine me, O God, and know my thoughts;
>   test me, and understand my misgivings.
> Watch lest I follow any path that grieves thee;
>   guide me in the (everlasting) ways.   (NEB)

Does the psalmist suddenly realize that wickedness is not as simple as that? What about *his* thoughts? What is it that God really does know about him? The word used for 'examine' (AV 'search') literally means 'dig deep'. Recently they were digging very deep near my home in the City where the Museum of London is being built, and as the weeks went by you could see layer upon layer of the past life of London being revealed by the excavation—a light stratum, and then a dark one. If God searches me, wondered the psalmist, digs deep into me—in the very way I have been praising—what will he find? What motives will be uncovered, what dark layers of failure and of resentment and the rest? If God were really to deal as abruptly with the wicked as I long, can I be sure of my own fate?

2

Songs of Questioning

Man today is unable to make up his mind what he really is. The modern world seems to speak with two voices about man, or it would be more sensible to say that man understands himself in two quite different ways in the light of all his new knowledge. The odd thing is that these two ways are quite contradictory of one another. They cannot *both* be true.

One way in which we understand man's role and status is that he is master of everything. Look back to earlier days, or to primitive societies tucked away even today from the impact of the modern world, and what do you find? Men believing that the gods or the spirits were in charge of everything. They determined whether disease would strike, or plague would abate and disappear. They would decide whether floods would come, causing the river to overflow bringing fertility or fearful damage. They would decide when fire would break out and destroy men's shelters and possessions. The only thing you could do was to try to influence or placate these spirits, by incantations and spells, by offerings of the sort likely to appease them. But it was the spirits that were in control of the world, and man at best was a suppliant at their court.

We understand things totally differently today. Man is master. Perhaps his mastery is not complete, for look at cancer and the sudden effects of typhoon or tidal wave – but the success of his mastery up to now suggests very powerfully that given time it

41

can be expanded. He does not go to the altar and the shrine to make sacrifices and murmur spells; he goes to the laboratory and works away with all the apparatus of science. He feeds his material into the computer and by-passes the laborious processes of calculation to learn the answers. Antibiotics and inoculation hold disease at bay, or cure it. The irrigation works provide for the river's overflow. The careful fire precautions and the fire brigade limit the power of fire to destroy.

The mastery may be partial, but that is because man's concentration, efficiency and industry are only partial. Give man time, and the rest will be mastered, too.

This is not something obscure and intellectual. It is something we all feel, and in a sense live by. If we are physically ill we send for the doctor, not for the priest. A friend of mine, a minister of a Surrey church, belatedly discovered that an old lady in his flock had been laid up for some weeks with a bad leg. 'Oh, if I'd known,' he said, 'I'd have come to visit you.' 'And what good would that have done my bad leg?' came the devastating reply. It is a remark singularly destructive of pastoral effort, but despite her years that lady was a woman of the modern age. She had sent not for the spiritual man, the man in touch with the spirits, but the specialist in the treatment of bad legs. This sense of man's mastery over the world is something that is built into us today.

But that is one voice in which the modern world speaks about man. But there is another, and it is quite contradictory. It says that man is not really master for he is really only a mechanism. He is purely what his gametes are. Gametes are the characteristics that we are given by heredity, by being the child of that father and that mother. We are programmed in fact, like a computer. It is a current affectation to blame the computer for everything, like astronomical gas bills and invoices that do not make sense, but of course it is quite silly to blame the computer. It has been programmed a certain way and is bound to produce the results that it does. In the same way, if man is programmed by his hereditary characteristics he cannot be blamed for anything that he does. It is as silly to blame him, to hold him morally responsible, as to blame the computer. Both are mechanisms. They are not in charge; they are not masters. They are wholly mastered by the instructions that have been fed or built into them.

More even than that. There is, it is suggested, something absurd in the picture of man strutting about congratulating himself upon his mastery of everything when he is only a two-legged creature on one small part of a minor planetary system amidst all the immensities of space and time that the astronomers have now revealed to us, at least to the degree to which the mind and imagination can really take them in. As David Edwards has put it in his book, *What is Real in Christianity?* (Collins Fontana 1972): 'In the astounding view of the universe which science provides, human life can so easily seem an insignificant accident among the galaxies.' If not as obviously a mechanism from this point of view, he looks little more than an accident, and a not very important one at that.

So we have this strange position, that two quite different answers seem to be given by our world and our experience today to the question, 'What is man?' Strangely, psalm 8, written though it was some twenty-seven centuries ago, is about just this issue. In fact the very words 'What is man?' appear in it.

Man did not need to wait till Eddington and Jeans, till Fred Hoyle, or Bernard Lovell with his Jodrell Bank telescope, to be awed by the heavens. From the earliest days of human history man has been awed by the sun and the moon and the celestial carpet of the skies. They have in fact filled him so much with awe and wonder that he has often made them the object of worship. The history of religion is full of sun-worshippers, moon-worshippers and those who adored the stars. More than this, the very sense of majesty and awe with which they filled him automatically raised the question 'What is man?'; where, in fact, can man fit into so vast and limitless a scheme of things?

Even if men in earlier days had no intellectual knowledge of of how limitless space was, and had in one sense a cosier view of the universe, seeing it in three-decker form, it must be recognized at the same time that men in earlier centuries lived lives less

43

insulated from the elements. Many of us can live in cities and be more aware of the street-lamps than the stars from one year's end to another. Man in earlier centuries went out into the night and felt the littleness of his life and his achievement under the stars.

Certainly the psalmist seems to have done that.

> When I look up at thy heavens, the work of thy fingers,
>   the moon and the stars set in their place by thee,
> what is man that thou shouldst remember him,
>   mortal man that thou shouldst care for him?

How telling is that seemingly slight change that the NEB translators have made in that last line, 'mortal man' . . . man who came from the dust and returns to the dust, mortal as he is, what does he matter in the light of the moon and the stars that will be there long after he has gone? The Jerusalem Bible also adds to the impact of the psalmist's cry, when it gives one phrase like this: 'What is man that you should spare a thought for him?'

It cannot really be put much more starkly than that. True, the psalmist saw the heavens as the work of God's fingers, and the modern man who has rejected religion will see them as no more than the immense product of casual and random forces. But if, in one sense, we are apt to be overwhelmed by the sheer *im*-personality of the vast universe, the believer in God faced a not dissimilar problem in wondering how the One who created all this could possibly spare a thought for man. Is man any more than an insignificant speck in all this? What is man indeed?

The answer that the psalmist gives to this candid questioning is startling. What is man? 'Thou hast made him little less than a god.' So both the NEB and Jerusalem read, in distinction from the familiar 'little lower than the angels' of the AV. The RSV went as far as 'God' with a capital 'G'. We need not enter into the technicalities which can support such variety. The real point is that the psalmist sees man as god-like, and some scholars firmly link the reference to the verse in Genesis, 'So God created man in his own image; in the image of God he created him.'

The psalmist for one thing is refusing to be overwhelmed by sheer physical material size. Men have always been in danger of confusing size with importance and value, and never more so than today.

The achievements of man today are and look impressive. Every traveller in modern Britain must be struck by the dominance of the landscape, as seen from train or car, by the great power stations, pumping electrical power into the grid to run thousands of factories. 'Power': it is the same word as the parson uses to speak of what can keep some insignificant little woman cheerful and courageous in some sorrow, or keep some nonentity of a young man from dipping his fingers into the till.

But in fact, if you look more closely, the first use of 'power' is quite ambiguous morally, that is, in terms of human well-being. The power can be going to factories making food or clothes, or healing drugs. But it can also be going to factories making poison gas, or bombs or bullets. The second power, the power to restrain people from evil, and succour and strengthen their spirits, is that which – if it flowed through enough people – could transform our world. There is no ambiguity about it. It is always positive. Sheer size is deceptive here. If man lacks inward power, the power to do right, the outwardly more impressive power spells disaster.

Merely to be overawed by appearances is to be guilty of an error of thinking, or allowing feeling and impression to overwhelm thought. The dinosaur, after all, must have looked far more powerful than unprotected man. There it was, almost incredibly vast, and armoured like a rhinoceros ten times over: by contrast there was little puny man with no more than a sparse covering of hair on his vulnerable skin. But it was man who survived, for it was man who had a mind, a power of reason and a consciousness that marked him off from the animals. There *is* that which is godlike about man. He has shown a power of reason, of foresight and planning, and of conscience that marks him off utterly from the rest of the animal world. He is in fact 'little less than a god'.

The psalmist goes on to mark the fact of man's dominion over the rest of the natural world.

> Thou makest him master over all thy creatures;
> thou hast put everything under his feet:
> all sheep and oxen, all the wild beasts,
> > the birds in the air and the fish in the sea,
> > and all that moves along the paths of ocean.

This is the poet's way of saying that the whole natural world is under man's mastery, and is intended by God so to be. That is the important point. It is not that man has shrugged off the fetters of religion, and now stands upright and in control of things. God intended that man should have this dominion, this mastery over the natural world. The immense efforts that man has made to control nature, to master his environment, are not an unspiritual aberration; they are man fulfilling his divine destiny.

So the psalmist refuses to be over-awed by size, overwhelmed by the vast spaces of the universe. He refuses to feel that he, a man, and his fellow-men are insignificant. Does this then mean that the Bible gives us an answer that cancels out one of the contradictory voices, which today answer the question, 'What is man?' Does it deny that man is an insignificant mechanism, and say that he is a master, and that is the end of it? No, that is wholly to misunderstand the answer of the psalmist.

What the psalmist affirms about man is part of his great affirmation about God. It is just as though he has been brooding long upon his theme and suddenly begins by breaking out into ecstatic exclamation, 'O Lord our sovereign, how glorious is thy name in all the earth!' The poem ends with the same ecstatic cry, 'O Lord our sovereign, how glorious is thy name in all the earth!'

The whole of what he has to say begins and ends with God. What is being said about man is what God intends man to be. There is not a word about man's fall or man's sin and failure. Not a word about what man's mastery over the world of nature can lead to. Today we are very aware of that. Perhaps in the last few years we have become more aware than ever of what an un-bridled and irresponsible mastery of nature can do. We are aware of it in terms of man's mastery over the raw material of the natural world – the atom. That threatens man's continued life as not even the most virulent and widespread plague could do in past centuries. We are aware of it, too, in terms of pollution of our environment and a reckless use of the earth's resources regardless of the needs of succeeding generations.

But, within the space of a short poem, this cannot be the theme of the psalmist. His theme is what God intends man to be. Yet even in this there are strong implications. It is what *God* intends man to be. Whatever man is, he is not a self-sufficient entity. Just because of the godlike powers that have been committed to him – in mind and reason and consciousness – that lead to such powerful mastery over his world, he needs to be aware of his two-fold relation. He is master over the beasts of the field and the birds of the air and the fish of the sea, master in fact over nature and environment, but he is also a son of God, made in God's image. Without awe and reverence the mastery put into his hands can only spell disaster.

The psalmist rightly refuses to be overawed by the stars, but he is deeply awed by the thought of God, and not of a God who is like one of those fabulous multi-millionaires so fantastically rich in possessions as to have a country house somewhere that he had staffed with servants and then totally lost all inkling of its existence. He is awed by the thought that the God who made the heavens made man and made him like himself. That awe, that adoring wonder, is the very stuff of worship. It exalts and humbles at the very same moment. It is an understanding of man that has hope for the future.

2 What Shall We Do With Fear?
Psalm 27, vv. 1–6

No theologian, it has been said, should dare to write a book offering the Christian answer to the problem of pain unless he has at least a raging headache at the time. Glib intellectual solutions can always be propounded by people who have not really felt the rub of the problem.

On the same principle it is reasonable to refuse to listen to recipes for the conquest of fear from a man who has never been gnawed by it. It is the man who has known, right within himself, what fear is, and what it can do to splinter life with a terrifying disintegration, and has then found some way of coping with it, that we want to hear.

We meet a man like that in the first part of psalm 27. (Probably, though not certainly, two psalms are joined together here, for not only the mood but the metre changes at verse seven. Our concern now is with the first six verses.)

If you look closely at those verses one of the things that comes home to you is how real the occasion, the cause, of fear is to his man. His very refusal to be afraid, the very vehemence of his confidence in God, is an awkward tribute to the power of things to make him afraid.

> The LORD is my light and my salvation;
> whom should I fear?
> The LORD is the refuge of my life;
> of whom then should I go in dread? (NEB)

Then his mind shifts to the evildoers who close in on him to devour him. The actual Hebrew is 'to eat up my flesh', but interestingly the RSV translates it as 'uttering slanders against me'. There is a warrant for that; it was a Hebrew metaphor for libelling someone. It is a telling point. Few things make us more afraid than to wonder what people are saying about us. The malicious tongue, even the thought that people might be 'saying things' about us, is a potent source of fear to most of us.

48

Then the psalmist says, 'If an army should encamp against me, my heart would feel no fear.' That is what is called hyperbole, a poet's great exaggeration. He is conjuring up the most fantastically awful thing that could happen to him, the thing really that makes his heart tremble, and still announces his confidence. Even if great numbers of armed men fell on him alone he cries that he would not be dismayed.

What a vivid imagination the psalmist has! But perhaps it was not that. These perhaps were some of the actual things that had happened to him. One commentator says that it is sheer autobiography. He had passed through times when people were speaking so cruelly of him that it was as if his flesh was being torn. He had been caught up in war; he had seen a mighty army encamped that dwarfed the puny forces of his own people.

The psalmist knew what fear was. He felt its cutting-edge; but he had found a way of conquest.

The Jerusalem Bible gives a simple heading to this psalm. It reads, 'In God's company there is no fear.' When are you most afraid? Isn't it when you are in your own company? Most of us remember when as children a most disturbing fear, perhaps in an empty house, could grip us. Every shadowed corner could shelter some lurking danger, every creak in the woodwork portend some fearful threat. But then another child comes, and all the fears disappear. How absurd! If there had been any substance in the fears what use would a child like yourself have been for dealing with the threat? But to be on your own was to be a prey to fears.

This is a parable in regard to larger and more justified fears. The more we are turned in on ourselves, the more we are eaten up with self-concern, the more a prey to fear we are. We see this most clearly when self-concern becomes really pathological, in the case of those sick people who have no concern for anything or anybody outside themselves. Fear can grip them in the most appalling way. They become terrified of disease. They begin to see all other people as a threat to them. These others will try to take what they have, or invade their privacy. They fear that they are going to become poor, though often such people have taken care to be amazingly well-cushioned against that contingency. And they fear death. They *are* like little children alone in a dark house, manufacturing alarms and fears from their own isolation from other people.

We all have some part of that sickness within us. So again and again the remedy for the grip of fear has been company.

But that heading in the Jerusalem Bible points us to something bigger than just human company. 'In God's company there is no fear.' What can this pious statement, 'In God's company there is no fear,' really mean?

Does it not mean that when there is a commitment to God's ways and purposes – when we try to do justly, and love mercy – we are brought into God's company? That after all is the third part of the great saying of Micah, 'to do justly, to love mercy, and to walk humbly with thy God'. For this means a commitment to that which is outside ourselves, a commitment to other people. When we make such a commitment we begin to be delivered, reach upon reach of our personalities, from that enclosed, stuffy, selfish darkness in which fears can breed. The sunshine begins to fill your life, and fresh breezes begin to blow through it, and in that atmosphere fears do not thrive. In the words of the psalmist God becomes your light and salvation and stronghold, and you find yourself able to cry out with him, 'Whom should I fear, of whom then should I go in dread?'

But there is something else, and you find it in the later part of these verses, the part that begins:

> One thing I ask of the LORD
>   one thing I seek:
> that I may be constant in the house of the LORD
>   all the days of my life,
> to gaze upon the beauty of the LORD
>   and to seek him in his temple.   (v.4 NEB)

At first glance this looks like rather a come-down, a come-down from the psalmist's thought that has moved in the large menacing secular world of war and violence. ('If an army should encamp against me . . . if armed men should fall upon me.') This seems escapist religion, withdrawing to the sanctuary where the occasions of fear cannot get at you, rather than staying where you are and defying them to do their worst. Does it not come under the condemnation of Milton's famous lines, 'I cannot praise a fugitive and cloistered virtue, unexercised and unbreathed, that never sallies out and sees her adversary, but slinks out of the race, where that immortal garland is to be run for, not without dust and heat'?

The feeling is stronger if you look at this psalm in the AV. 'One thing have I desired of the Lord, that will I seek after; that I may dwell in the house of the Lord all the days of my life . . .' The words are lovely, but the meaning suggests only escapist retreat. The NEB's 'to be constant' at least suggests a regular worshipper rather than someone who has gone to roost for good in church and does not intend to come out of it and let life get at him again.

Of course, the NEB reflects the truer meaning. In fact no one did live in the temple. And when the AV went on 'in the secret of his tabernacle shall he hide me', the literalist could object that only the High Priest was allowed in the tabernacle, and that but once a year. The whole thing is poetry, some of it moving poetry when you think of how words like 'he will hide me under the cover of his tent' (NEB) use the picture of the Bedouin sheik giving to his guest, even in the bitterest blood feud, a quite inviolable sanctuary.

The psalmist's point is that he yearns for such constancy in the worship of the people of God that the sense of God's presence and power shall become a constant and sustaining experience. Then he says, 'I can raise my head high above the enemy all about me.' He has not withdrawn, he has armoured himself against fear by this sense of the presence of God.

We must be careful to be real and honest here. The sense of the presence of God cannot be constant in the sense of being consciously there all the minutes of our life. Our consciousness is busy, and ought to be busy, with other tasks. William Temple said something to the effect that a bus-driver who was saying his prayers when driving his bus was doing wrong. Our concentration should be upon the tasks which are our duty, or even upon the enjoyments which are our pleasure. But–and here is the all-important point–our whole tackling of our duties, and our whole choosing of our pleasures should owe most to an underlying sense of the presence of God in all life. One wise man said that people could argue for ever as to whether it is possible for mortal men to have a really unbroken communion with God, but the point for most of us was much more whether it needs to be as broken and intermittent as it is. Maclaren says: 'The Australian rivers in a drought present a picture of the Christian life of far too many of us–a stagnant, stinking pool here, a stretch of blinding gravel there; another little drop of water a mile away, then a long line of foul-smelling mud, and then another shallow pond. Why! it ought to run in a clear stream that has a scour in it and that will take all the filth off the surface.'

The same writer says: 'Many desires are unsatisfied because conduct does not correspond to desires.' You cannot seek the company of God if you want at the same time to company with those things that you would hide from God if you could. If we desire the sense of God's presence to be less fitful, more real in the rubs and pains of daily life, it must be sought. The psalmist wanted that, and he knew that there was a prerequisite for it:

> to gaze upon the beauty of the Lord
> and to seek him in his temple.

There was a time and a place for renewal of the sense of the presence of God, a time for concentration upon *that* and that alone. You cannot do that in the middle of life's duties; then your concentration must be elsewhere. But worship means such renewal, renewal of a sense which can be there at deeper levels of life, guiding motives, protecting against invasion by evil, and delivering from fear.

3 Does God Care?
Psalm 77

If I were asked to say what was Shakespeare's most memorable line I would have no difficulty of personal choice. It would be that simple, unforgettable image in *Macbeth*,

> Sleep that knits up the ravelled sleeve of care.

Paradoxically it is a line that most often occurs to me during a sleepless night.

Psalm 77 is about a sleepless night, but not the casual desertion of a man by sleep but the time when a man's life has had its fabric ravelled away by care.

I can remember when I first became aware of this psalm. It was in a film of Rembrandt's life made well over thirty years ago. Charles Laughton played the artist, who was portrayed returning home after a long absence during which he had lived in a style remote from the simple pieties of his Dutch home. It is evening as he returns, and the time for family prayers. They hand the returned wanderer the old Bible, and he turns the pages until he comes to this psalm. Then the wonderful voice of Laughton reads the words, as though they were a passage of Rembrandt's autobiography:

> Will the Lord cast off for ever? and will
> he be favourable no more?
> Is his mercy clean gone for ever? doth his
> promise fail for evermore?
> Hath God forgotten to be gracious? hath he in
> anger shut up his tender mercies?

I found the psalm and memorized it. The cadences of the Authorized Version are imprinted on my memory. So it was a harsh test to which to put the New English Bible, to see what this great personal favourite was like. In fact it achieves beauty to a remarkable degree, but it also has a telling impact through simplicity.

Could anything make clearer than this translation the horror of that kind of sleepless night which comes not just from a little overtiredness, or some other passing thing, but because a man is at the end of his tether, because nerves are stretched out to snapping point, because both the roof seems to be falling in, and the ground beneath his feet seems to be giving way? The feverish feeling—

> I lay sweating and nothing would cool me;

The stubborn refusal of anything that would soften the martyr-dom—

> I refused all comfort.

And the ghastly time when what should be the source of comfort becomes an aggravation of anguish—

> When I called God to mind, I groaned;
> as I lay thinking, darkness came over my spirit.

And into the over-active mind there crowd the remorseless images of past failure, of times when you have been silly and embarrassing, of acts of shame, of jobs left untackled until you cannot face them.

How much more telling for all this than the AV's

> I have considered the days of old, the
> years of ancient times

is the NEB's

> My thoughts went back to times long past,
> I remembered forgotten years;

It is not history that the anguished man has been brooding on; it is his own past. The debris of shortcomings that have piled up across the years has become a great heap of rubble that towers over him, about to collapse and bury all possibility of happiness for ever. Or, to use another image, the fevered memory lowers a net into the depths of forgotten years and drags up a catch of failure, and foolishness.

It is at *this* point that God becomes not a comfort but an

aggravation. Isn't it wonderful that the Bible is so honest a book? I have always questioned what used to be told us in our theological colleges, that we should only speak of our certainties and not of our doubts. Had the men who so advised us never read the book of psalms? Had they not even noticed that the psalmists tell not only of their doubts but of their distress to the point of denial? The psalmists do this, too, at the point which is always sharpest for the man of faith, or would-be-faith. That point is whether God really cares–

> Will the Lord reject us for evermore
> and never again show favour?

And the N E B brings in a heartbreaking irony in the next line:

> Has his unfailing love now failed us utterly?

The thought of God's enduring, unfailing love is one of the great themes of the psalms. Now the bitter question has to be asked, whether the unfailing love has proved not to be true–has the unfailing love of God, when it came to the pinch, failed utterly?

So we come to the tenth verse of the psalm, where the Hebrew as it appears in the manuscripts is virtually unintelligible, and the sense has to be reconstructed. Earlier versions did not really achieve this successfully. The Jerusalem Bible tackles it boldly, but perhaps too colloquially–

> 'This' I said then 'is what distresses me:
> that the power of the Most High is no longer what it was.'

The meaning is clear, but there is a strong smell of bathos about this. The N E B rises to this difficult task with superb power–

> 'Has his right hand', I said, 'lost its grasp?
> Does it hang powerless, the arm of the most High?'

Hasn't that caught the agony of doubt exactly, and with an unforgettable image? Here is colloquial force without any bathos, for we do talk colloquially about a man losing his grip. When we are sunk in doubt we wonder whether God's power 'to grasp this sorry scheme of things entire' has gone. And this vivid picture is reinforced by the sombre image of the arm of God hanging powerless and paralysed.

But if all that this psalm did was to etch unforgettably the picture of our doubt, and how all this can assail us when we are at our lowest in the dead of the night, it would be of literary and human value, but without any religious message. If all the NEB did was to restore the picture by dissolving away the obscurities which change of language and inadequate understanding of the original have brought to darken the picture, it would add to our depression. But the glory of the psalm is that it shows how a man came out of this state. Part of the value, indeed a very great part of the value, is that the state is portrayed so unforgettably and with such convincing power, that we can say 'Yes, that's what it feels like!' But the glory is that it tells how the man emerged from that darkness and dereliction.

How did he?

> But then, O LORD, I call to mind thy deeds;
> I recall thy wonderful acts in times gone by.
> > I meditate upon thy works
> > and muse on all that thou hast done.

One old commentator says on this part of the psalm, 'Memory is on God's side.' That's a fine phrase, a memorable phrase, a well-rounded phrase. But *is it true*? I began by quoting from *Macbeth*, 'Sleep that knits up the ravelled sleeve of care.' But the same play has something to say about memory when Macbeth pleads with the doctor on behalf of his wife for a medicine and a surgery which do not exist:

> Cure her of that:
> Canst thou not minister to a mind diseas'd,
> Pluck from the memory a rooted sorrow,
> Raze out the written troubles of the brain,
> And with some sweet oblivious antidote
> Cleanse the stuff'd bosom of that perilous stuff
> Which weighs upon the heart?

It was in the night, whether in terrible dreams or sleeplessness, that the memory of what they had done drove Macbeth and his queen to distraction and terror. 'Pluck from the memory a rooted sorrow . . .' Is memory really to be described simply as on God's side? It is not. After all, in the experience of the psalmist it was partly the exercise of the same faculty that had brought him to despair.

> . . . as I lay thinking, darkness came over my spirit . . .

> My thoughts went back to times long past,
>   I remembered forgotten years;
> all night long I was in deep distress,
> as I lay thinking, my spirit was sunk in despair.   (NEB)

Part of the horror of such an experience is that memory works overtime, but works with a tragic selectiveness. People are always accusing the religious man of looking at life through rosy-tinted spectacles, as the saying goes. But the worried man, the sleepless man, the over-wrought man looks through dark glasses that shed an artificial gloom over everything. Or to put it in another, and perhaps better picture, does not the memory of the man under strain have a mesh that lets through all manner of niggling, small, irritating, distressing things, while keeping out the big reassuring things?

What the psalmist does is to turn to those big things. He thinks of the holiness of God. That again is new light from the NEB. The AV gives it most unhelpfully, 'Thy way, O God, is in the sanctuary': but it is not God in the sanctuary we need; it is God out in life, active in our lives. The NEB says simply:

> O God, thy way is holy.

And the great evidence for this is redemption:

> With thy strong arm–

(where is the hand that has lost its grasp, now, where the arm that hangs powerless?)

> With thy strong arm thou didst redeem thy people,
> the sons of Jacob and Joseph . . .

and the same thought of the salvation at the time of the Exodus appears to close the poem after the striking passage about God riding the storm:

> Thou didst guide thy people like a flock of sheep,
> under the hand of Moses and Aaron.

This was the great evidence to which the Jews looked back as showing the purpose of God, and affirming that his unfailing love was a reality. God was Guide and God was Redeemer, no matter how troubled the present time.

It is this that you find Paul saying at the close of the eighth chapter of Romans. He begins with the great challenge, 'Who shall separate us from the love of God?' And he reels off the whole grim catalogue, all the suffering which perplexes the man of faith – hunger, nakedness, catastrophe, war, and hardest of all, persecution, the suffering which comes just because a man is trying to be a faithful servant of God. He then dares to say that the Christian man is more than conqueror in all this. Why? When memory has been bold enough to recall all the evil things that can happen, what can it dredge up that will counterbalance that grisly collection? Only one thing – the love of God shown in Christ Jesus our Lord.

It is the same thing: God as Redeemer shown in mighty acts of love. The Israelite turned his thoughts back to the bondage of Egypt, the Red Sea and the Wilderness, that had led to the Promised Land. The Christian turns his mind back to Jesus of Nazareth, his Cross and his Resurrection. And, if he is wise, too, he makes a deliberate effort to recall the gracious acts of God in his own life.

When we have our sleepless nights, or their equivalent, when despair begins to get us in its grip, when memory only brings failures and foolishness to torment us, we can try the psalmist's recipe. There is a simple word for it; it is thanksgiving. He thanks God for what he has done. He sets memory to wholesome and reinvigorating tasks.

4   Is God Found in Nature?
Psalm 121

By a happy chance when the bi-centenary of the birth of Words-worth was being celebrated I was able to be at worship in Gras-mere parish church where he was married, and where, in the churchyard, he lies buried. When it came to the sermon-time the pulpit was occupied by Professor Basil Willey who, in view of what follows, it is interesting to note was one of the panel of literary advisers who guided the final form of the New English Bible. He spoke of how people had often quoted the opening verse of psalm 121 as justifying the message that Wordsworth had found in the loveliness of the hills of Cumberland and Westmorland. 'I will lift up mine eyes unto the hills, from whence cometh my help.' He went on to say that this was quite un-justifiable, for here the AV was misleading. He turned to the NEB which had got it right. This is how it goes in the new translation:

> If I lift up my eyes to the hills,
>   where shall I find help?

It has become a question. It is a question that receives its answer in the next verse:

> Help comes only from the LORD,
>   maker of heaven and earth.

Here is new light from the NEB indeed. For how often, whether in regard to Wordsworth or not, has this psalm been used to justify some kind of nature worship, the religion of those caricatured by Monsignor Ronald Knox when he described the 'Blue-domers', worshipping under the blue dome of heaven, 'unseared by the fiery blast of pulpit eloquence, and untried by the material test of the collection plate'. That kind of nature worship has a very great appeal to us today. We are in revolt against institutions, so if we can worship God in nature and not in the church this is a most satisfying release. We are in revolt against written codes and inherited wisdom, so again if we can find God in mountain and moor and sky and throw away that black book with its two hoary old testaments, what could be a more attractive proposition? We are in revolt against history, against any concern with the past, so again if we can turn to the loveliness of the natural world as it confronts our senses, and reject all concern with Moses and Pharaoh, and with Jesus and Pilate, and all the rest, we are on the right track.

I will lift up mine eyes to the hills, and to the rolling seas, and to the wide sweep of the moor and the forest—all this makes sense to us. We may not exactly worship these natural phenomena, but there is that in them which kindles the imagination, and swells the heart, and somehow mysteriously uplifts our sense of what life is about. Of all this sense of awe and wonder in nature Wordsworth is the prophet.

But honesty, even in that commemorative address about the poet, compelled the speaker to affirm that the support of this psalm could not be claimed for such an attitude. And we must in fact recognize that the claim to find God exclusively through nature leaves us with a very strange religion indeed. Suppose, asked Professor Willey, Wordsworth had been born in the depths of the steamy heat of the jungle in the Amazon basin; would this not have given a different notion of God from the gentle hills and lovely lakes of his actual native country? Can we be as selective in our choice of the aspects of nature that reflect God? Is not nature's message—taken on its own—a very ambiguous one? I am not thinking only of Tennyson's often quoted observation about 'nature red in tooth and claw'—the apparent brutality of the process of natural selection—but even that some parts of nature are dreary, and even repellent.

We find God in the sublimer aspects of nature because we have already found him somewhere else. I remember a remarkable sermon preached at the City Temple by Dr Howard Williams during a festival of flowers. There was he looking out from the pulpit to a church that was a glorious glow of masses of flowers, moving from the dark blues and reds of the side chapels and rear windows to the gold and white of the sanctuary. The whole church building cried a paeon of praise of the glory and beauty of nature. And what he said from the pulpit was that you would never find God in nature unless you had first found him in history. It seemed wantonly perverse, *but he was right*. For had he said, 'This is where you will find God', the sceptic could have said, 'But I can fill your building with the rankest of weeds, with poisonous plants, with flowers whose seeds will drug a man into insensibility.' And would we then have said simply, 'You can find God here'?

When we look at nature at its most lovely and sublime we find it sacramental of a God whom we already know to be beauty, truth and goodness because he has revealed himself to us in other ways. When we sing:

> Yes, God is good: in earth and sky,
>   From ocean depths and spreading wood,
> Ten thousand voices seem to cry,
>   'God made us all, and God is good.'

This is a perfectly reasonable poetic fancy for Christians, for what we are doing then is seeing nature as sacramental of a God who has already revealed his goodness to us. On its own, not illuminated from elsewhere, the message of the natural world is nothing like so unambiguous.

What the psalmist does is to find his confidence in God's care of himself in the simple thought of what he has done for his people, the people of Israel.

> How could he let your foot stumble?
>   How could he, your guardian, sleep?
> The guardian of Israel
>   never slumbers, never sleeps.

This is a psalm for pilgrims. The imagery, or pictures, of the psalm are those that are natural for people on a journey through rough country with none of the prepared ways that the modern traveller expects. They are the pictures of a traveller in the east– when the sun is not, as here, something to be pathetically hoped for but to be feared. It is a fiery blast threatening death, not a gentle warmth drying out the rained-on traveller; when the moon is thought, after the fashion of simple people in those parts even today, to be the source of all manner of diseases; when a stumbling foot leads not to at worse a sprained ankle, but to a plunge to death into a ravine.

When it was first written this psalm would probably have been understood quite literally as proclaiming the preservation of the traveller who believed in God from the dangers of the way. Certainly we could not so use it today. The fact that a man is a devout believer does not ensure that the aircraft he travels on will not be sabotaged or fail. When metal fatigue tragically wrecked those Comets with great loss of life we are not to imagine that no one aboard believed in God, for he would not have suffered them to 'stumble'.

Even in the later use of the psalm before Christ's coming there must surely have been some movement away from a purely literal interpretation. When Christ came we know that he stumbled, he stumbled under the weight of the cross. And far from God not letting his foot so stumble it was his obedience to God that put that weight on his shoulders. Far from the sun not striking him by day, he was nailed there on a cross precisely so that the sun could strike him with its terrible blast of heat and bring him to agonizing death. And it was the moonlight that had brought him the agony of Gethsemane, the apathy of his sleeping followers and the betrayal by one of his dearest friends. You cannot set the 121st psalm on the lips of Jesus in those days of crisis and death and read it literally. The securities of which it speaks have to be found not in deliverance from the common experiences of mankind but in a sense that God guards us from the things that would destroy our true life. In *this* sense, 'The Lord will guard you against all evil.'

It was surely in this sense that God had been the guardian of Israel. Any interpretation of Israel's history as 'roses, roses all the way' shrivels in contact with reality. If God's guardianship was to be expressed in that literal way of deliverance from any kind of physical challenge or harm, why did he not put his chosen people at least on some remote island in the South Seas, where the ravages of nature would be reduced to the minimum, and where enemies would be few? Instead of this he led them to a promised land which was just a bridge, the narrow fertile strip between sea and desert, the ends of which rested in the great empires of the era. So across the land – the *promised* land – it was obvious that empires would tramp, and the people in it would be in the cockpit of history. What a strange guardian of Israel!

No, we cannot with profit read this psalm as a man with more primitive ideas would have read it – with God offering an all-risks policy for travellers. I think we get the clue in the last verse:

> The Lord will guard your going and your coming,
> now and for evermore.

Whatever experiences life may bring – and the final experience of death – the believing man knows that he is in the hands of One who is always on duty. The experiences through which Israel had lived, slavery in Egypt, flight before the armies of Pharaoh, seemingly ceaseless wanderings in the inhospitable wilderness, the struggle to find a lodging place in Canaan, the successive empires that had trampled them down, exiled their leaders and destroyed their cities, all had somehow revealed to them a guardian God. When countries like Egypt that had seemed to be always victorious and strong were worshipping cats the sense of a caring God who guarded Israel's going and coming had held them in thrall.

And a strong element in their understanding of God, or to put it the right way round, God's revelation of himself is represented by that strange phrase –

> The guardian of Israel
> never slumbers, never sleeps.

The two-fold 'never' of the NEB seems to make it more emphatic. It may originally have referred to the notion that the nature deities who were worshipped on the tops of the hills in shrines – If I lift up my eyes to the hills, where shall I find help? – were thought of as sleeping in the way that nature seems to sleep through the long dark months of winter. If this is so then, of course, we have here a further sharpening of the contrast between a mere worship of nature and the worship of the guardian God.

What probably says more to us is that the phrase about an unsleeping God poetically expresses the great conviction of the Bible that God is living and active. He has not just made the world and turned to rest and sleep. He is not thereafter just to be found in the world he has made, a god of nature. He is above all active and living in the lives of men and women. We find his unsleeping activity in the lives of men and the movements of history. We cannot say of human history at any point, 'Oh, God was asleep then.' He is *always* at work. We think of today as being a day of no faith, or irreligion. And we can slip into the notion, from that, of thinking that God is not at work in days like ours. But God 'never slumbers, never sleeps' says the psalmist. Every era is an era of God's activity.

So we come back to where we began:

> If I lift up my eyes to the hills,
> where shall I find help?

God is only found in the hills, or any other beauty of nature, as we find them to be sacramental of the God we already know. Only recently did I learn the fourth line in that poem by Elizabeth Barrett Browning, the first three lines of which are a familiar quotation:

> Earth's crammed with heaven,
> And every common bush afire with God;
> But only he who sees takes off his shoes,
> The rest sit round it and pluck blackberries.

Probably the compilers of anthologies of religious verse find the fourth line a little bathetic. But how much it adds to the force of what the poet is saying! A friend once told me of being in the country with a man who had made a great fortune in the City of London. They passed a glorious cornfield, the breeze on it making it like some rolling golden sea. My friend exclaimed with delight, and said 'Look!' 'My!–I wonder how much an acre the farmer will get for that,' was her companion's exclamation. For her it was afire with God; for him it was money to be harvested.

In the same way the action of God in a man's life, or in the movement of history will be seen by those with eyes ready to see, and dismissed by those without the gift of sight. So the movement of long oppressed peoples towards freedom and independence is to the man of faith proof that God does not sleep in this age that we are pleased to call irreligious; to the selfish man it is just a disturbance of the *status quo* in which he happens to be privileged, and therefore to be described as the devil's work, if he could exert himself to believe in anything as definite as a devil.

Help to faith does not come from the hills, or from the movement of history unless we have been found by God already. The psalmist had been found by God in the dealings that God had had with his people. The Christian has been found by God in Jesus of Nazareth. So found he can see God in the hills and the seas, in the hearts of men and the tides of history, and still affirm

Help comes only from the Lord.

3

Songs of Strong Comfort

1 Recipe for Serenity
Psalm 34

The honest answer to the question, 'What do you want out of life?' for most of us would just be, 'I want to be happy.' As Artur Weiser said, commenting on the psalm which is our theme, psalm 34, 'Every human being is on the look-out for happiness.' That word 'look-out' is admirable; it describes it exactly. We have an eye cocked for the sight of possible happiness.

The psalmist says that. In the old version it is expressed with beauty, but perhaps with little immediate impact. 'What man is he that desireth life, and loveth many days, that he may see good?' It suggests that the pursuit of virtue is what most people want. But turn to the newer translations and you get a much more down-to-earth impression that corresponds with what we know of ourselves. 'Which of you delights in life and desires a long life to enjoy all good things?' (v. 12 NEB), or, even more starkly in TEV, 'Would you like to enjoy life? Do you want long life and happiness?' That is on our wave-length. That is the language we really use. 'Which of you . . . ?' Every single one of us.

Yes, that is on our wave-length, but we also know (the moment we stop being naive) that it is not really as easy as that. You can be on the look-out for happiness, and think you have recognized it, only to discover that it turns out to be nothing of the sort. How many people have thought that happiness consisted in having a lot of things–'enjoying all good things' to use the psalmist's words–only to find that somehow the savour goes out of them when there is nothing to do but enjoy them. How many people, especially and understandably hard-pressed people overburdened with work, think that happiness will lie in total leisure, early retirement from responsibility, only to find that when leisure is not a treat but a constant state it does not yield happiness. Happiness is not easy to recognize, other things can disguise themselves as happiness, and our mental look-out can be mistaken.

That is one of the problems, but only one. We have to stop being naive, and when we do that we recognize that it is a rare life indeed that has not got to cope with disagreeable and profoundly disturbing experiences. We may want long life and happiness, but we are not going to get just what we want. Any recipe for living worth having has got effectively to cope with all *that* side of life, its disturbing and distressing element, illness, stress, sorrow, frustration and the like. In fact what we want is not so much a recipe for happiness, but a recipe for serenity, the power to live through the varied experiences of life, happy and wretched, with a real inner serenity that enables us to cope. Otherwise the darker side of life shadows all else and mars such happiness as we might enjoy.

It is just this that psalm 34 is about; it is a recipe for serenity.

It is what in cooking circles is called, I believe, a tested recipe. I was entertained a few years ago to see a correction which appeared in the home hints page of a Sunday newspaper; it was to the effect that the word 'dessertspoonful' of baking powder should have read 'teaspoonful'. The imagination readily conjured up what strange sights must have been seen in the kitchens of prentice cooks in the intervening weeks. The recipe as printed was untested. But, by contrast, I remember a young woman who read Leslie Weatherhead's book *Prescription for Anxiety*. She had her own problems of anxiety. She was a claustrophobic. She exclaimed as she read the book, 'This man knows what it feels like.' It was a tested recipe.

So is the psalmist's. His song begins with an exclamation of praise, 'I will bless the Lord continually; his praise shall be always on my lips,' and a summons to others to join him in praise: 'O glorify the Lord with me, and let us exalt his name together.' Both the exclamation and the summons arise from a deep personal experience through which he has passed.

> I sought the LORD's help and he answered me;
> He set me free from all my terrors . . .

> Here was a poor wretch who cried to the Lord;
> he heard him and saved him from all his troubles.   (NEB)

We do not know what it was that this man had to face, whether it was desperate sickness or sorrow, or just that devastating sense of meaningless and seemingly unbased depression that can make greater havoc of a man's life than any identifiable trouble. There is a significant reference to his terrors which suggests it might have been the last-named. Perhaps it is good that we do not know the problem in any detail, for the details would be different from our own – as every man's must be – but the experience of appalling inward turmoil is the same. That is universal experience. The root of the anxiety may not be revealed, but its hideous harvest in the devastation of happiness all too many of us know.

And this man had found that turning to God had given him serenity, the deliverance from his terrors. He had found the secret of liberation. It does not mean that he believes that the man of faith is exempt from trouble. In one way a superficial reading of the psalm might suggest that. But look at the verse, 'The good man's misfortunes may be many, the Lord delivers him out of them all.' In one of those later verses there is even the suggestion that it may be the very experiences that destroy a man's self-confidence that open him to receive the serenity that can never finally be found in himself. The NEB strikingly translates it:

> The LORD is close to those whose courage is broken
> and he saves those whose spirit is crushed.

Where the AV speaks of a broken heart the newer translation talks of a broken courage. Perhaps the breaking of our courage is

68

a later stage than the breaking of our hearts. Many a man and woman can go on with sorrow having broken the heart; it is when experiences pile up and the courage to face them all breaks, too, that a man is desolate.

All this, it seems, had been the dark valley through which this man had passed, and the message he had to give was that he had deliverance from his anxiety and serenity and peace by turning to God. There is a verse that comes in between the autobiographical verses, the ones that begin 'I sought the Lord's help . . .' and 'This poor man cried, and the Lord heard him.' In the old version it seems a curious intrusion, lovely as it is. It reads, 'They looked unto him, and were lightened: and their faces were not ashamed.' Who are these intrusive 'they'? Most modern translations prefer another reading which yields a different sense. 'Look to him and be radiant' (RSV), 'Look towards him and shine with joy' (NEB). Thus the verse becomes a spontaneous outburst that interrupts the man's account of his own experience and sheds immense light on it. Perhaps the Jerusalem Bible does best of all when it gives it as 'Every face turned to him grows brighter.'

For what is in fact our experience when we pass through our periods of deep inner turmoil, for whatever cause? We look in on ourselves. We can see it clearly when other people do it. 'He's turned in on himself,' we say, shaking our heads. When our inner turmoil is a merely physical one we naturally find ourselves thinking about our stomachs, the pains and rumblings therein. We do the same thing when the inner turmoil is nervous, mental, spiritual. We turn in on ourselves.

The recipe that the psalmist has tested and passes on is to turn from ourselves: 'Look towards God and shine with joy,' and he gives the guarantee, 'Every face turned to him grows brighter.' As we look in on ourselves at such points in our lives we are looking at darkness, and we grow darker by doing it. As we look towards the source of all light and peace we reflect light and peace as that which is turned to the sun inevitably reflects its rays.

This must have meant something definite and concrete. It meant a making time for worship, for meditation, for deliberate thinking about God and his goodness. He had tried it out. I remember going to a coffee party once run by an eccentric hostess. I found her in a corner of one of the crowded rooms drinking tea. 'I didn't like the look of the coffee,' she confessed. She wasn't risking it. I didn't after that! But what is it the psalmist exclaims – in words that have naturally been caught up into the communion service of the Christian church, 'O taste and see that the Lord is good: blessed is the man that trusteth in him'? That is the right language for a recipe! Take a spoonful and see how good it is. TEV boldly paraphrases it, losing the impact of 'tasting', but driving home the basic meaning, 'Find out for yourself how good the Lord is!'

Finally, look at the closing part of the psalm, the part that actually follows the verse with which we began: 'Which of you delights in life and desires a long life to enjoy all good things?' For one of the great virtues of this psalm is that it gets down to cases, as it were; it is practical. And, thank heaven, life does not consist in crises of anxiety and turmoil, even though those may be the gravest test of whether faith works, and the sharpest challenge to our happiness. How should a man tackle life normally? That is the question that in effect our poet is asking.

The point at which he begins is interesting. It comes again and again in the 'wisdom' literature, as it is called in the Old Testament of which Proverbs is the best-known example. It may seem a rather pedestrian point: 'Keep your tongue from evil and your lips from uttering lies.' Be honest and straightforward. But can God do for any man what he wants to do if a man does not honour the truth? It is desperately hard to help any man whose life has become a morass of evasions and lies. You do not know where you are with him. No man can know serenity who is not straightforward.

Then come five words that form a simple but far-reaching command. 'Seek peace, and pursue it.' 'Desire peace and do your best to have it' (TEV). Want it, and do something about getting it. Peace here is a widely embracing word. It contains both the thought of our inward peace, our inner well-being on the one hand, and our right relationships with others on the other hand. They are not really separate; they belong together, for no man can have real serenity who has broken relationships with others. Let a man's heart seethe with jealousy, resentment, bitterness towards others and he can no more know peace in his heart than a man with indigestion can know peace in his stomach.

'Desire peace and do your best to have it.' You want serenity, yes, but do you do your best to have it? Do you still want to go on 'nursing your wrath to keep it warm' in Burns' expressive phrase, nourishing your bitterness against someone for what he did or said about you? If you do you cannot have serenity, you cannot have peace. You may want it, but you are not *pursuing* it.

And beyond this there is all that is contained in the words, unattractive to us, but the very heart of what the Old Testament means by 'wisdom' – 'the fear of the Lord'. The introduction to this whole part of the psalm lies just there:

> Come, my children, listen to me:
> I will teach you the fear of the LORD.
> Which of you delights in life
> and desires a long life to enjoy all good things?

Delight and enjoyment for this man lie in learning the fear of the Lord. We have got this 'fear' business wrong. It does not mean terror of an angry God. It means, 'the manner of life which is sensitive to the all-important fact of God' (Eaton). It means a life which loves the things that God loves. This is an essential consequence of that looking to God and catching something of his radiance. We know this in human life. If we come to revere someone we know, we speak of 'looking up' to him. And as a consequence this means our admiring the things he admires, caring for the things he cares for and so on. 'Reverence', not 'fear' as we normally understand it, is the clue here.

This means that God is not just someone that we look to for help in the day of crisis, when inner turmoil and distress shatter our lives. Not that way lies the recipe for serenity. It is a way of life. We may come to learn it in the day of trouble, but it matters greatly that we should live by it afterwards.

What do you want out of life? 'I want to be happy.' But happiness is really a by-product of something else, of living by the values that make for happiness. Therein is delight and the enjoyment of all good things.

2   The Sheltering God
Psalm 46

If chaos should come again – what then? In the odd way in which experiences come together, during the week in which I was studying psalm 46 I was relaxing at bedtime with a novel which had as its theme the inability to de-fuse a nuclear bomb in mid-air when the use of it to deter had been effective, and it should have been returned safely to its base in an English airfield. I write 'relaxing', but only in the sense that it was not as intellectually strenuous as the study of scripture. Nervously it was far more taxing, for the novel brought home to you that while it was fiction its substance was reality. These devices exist, and when this one could not be defused the problem was to find some 40,000 square miles of the earth's surface on which it could be dropped without slaughtering people in their millions. That problem is fact. Chaos can come again, and the earth be as though there had been no act of creation, or no rising of the proud mind of man from the primaeval slime.

> . . . when the earth gives way,
> when mountains tumble into the depths of the sea,
> and its waters roar and seethe,
> the mountains tottering as it heaves.

That is the psalmist's picture – in the vivid words of the Jerusalem Bible translation – of chaos come again. It is, of course, the reversal of that picture of creation with which our Bible begins, the picture of God brooding on the waters of chaos and causing the firmament and the dry land to appear. For chaos you had a cosmos, a world brought into being and kept in being and ordered by God. But what if chaos should come again? We know now that the psalmist was drawing on widespread myths in the Near East, because discoveries have been made by the archaeologists called the Ras Shamra tablets. There in the underworld were the waters of chaos, symbolized by the dragon, Timiat. Supposing the waters were to rise again?

That was their way of picturing, or rather of deeply feeling, that chaos could come again. We have our own understanding. Chaos will not rise from the underworld but fall from the sky if man's destructive fears gain ascendancy.

But never mind the picture; what if it should happen?

> God is our shelter, our strength,
> ever ready to help in time of trouble,
> so we shall not be afraid when the earth gives way,
> when mountains tumble into the depths of the sea,
> and its waters roar and seethe,
> the mountains tottering as it heaves.

If chaos should come again—what then? God, just that. God is there, cries the psalmist, setting his words, too, on the lips of God's worshipping people, God is there. Though I have called this study 'The Sheltering God' do not let us picture the psalm thus described as some cosy presentation of an escapist religion. It is quite the reverse. It is a psalm in which the test of faith is pushed to its ultimate limit. What if chaos should come again, with the centre of the earth giving way and the mountains tumbling into the pit thus made, and the foaming waters seething and roaring? What of your faith then?

It is really made up of three stanzas, a fact obscured by the omission of the refrain at the end of the first. In the second stanza a more immediate cause for profound alarm and disturbance of spirit is set out with force. It is described as 'the roaring of nations and tottering of kingdoms', or 'nations are terrified, kingdoms are shaken'. If the thought of chaos come again refers to the end of all things, this refers to present disorder, the shaking of the world as it is by international dissension and the collapse of order amongst the nations. Not the nuclear end of all things but Vietnam, the Middle East, Northern Ireland, the Cold War . . . What can a man hold on to in a world like this, let alone if, the world were to come to an abrupt end? In fact this is the sharper question, for a man might well feel – and perhaps we fatalistically do – that if chaos and destruction on that scale were to come again it would not matter, for he would end with the world. Only the man of faith looks beyond chaos for continuing life. But all men have to wonder by what to live in a world that seems to be destroying itself.

This is emphatically no cosy piece of religious escapism. It poses the questions both of present and ultimate horror with a grim vigour. But it is emphatic in the answer; it is that God is a citadel, a high stronghold, who is unshaken by the raging either of nations or of the waters of chaos. This is supremely a song of confidence in God, and it spells out the reason for it. Up to now you may say we have been seeing how the psalmist feels and describes the *challenge* to confidence, the things that can shatter a man's faith. But now we move on to the secret of his confidence.

After the crashing of the waves of the chaotic sea and the tumbling of the mountains from their places it seems strange suddenly to move to 'There is a river, the streams whereof do make glad the city of God.' In fact, a more literal translation would be 'Lo, a river . . .', the river pops up as abruptly as that.

> There is a river that brings joy to the city of God,
>   to the sacred house of the Most High.
> God lives in the city, and it will never be destroyed;
>   at early dawn he will come to its help.   (TEV)

Ah, we may say, a description of Jerusalem, and a pretty fanciful one at that. 'Never be destroyed'; but it was! 'God lives in the city'; that was the crude thought that led the Jews to boast proudly of their indestructible city, but if fell! But let us not be too swift in our turning away from this as an outdated picture. In fact this psalm, most scholars believe, was written after the exile. That is *after* the destruction of Jerusalem, and the razing of its Temple! But in any case it could hardly be the literal physical city of Jerusalem that was being described, for uniquely amongst the great cities of the ancient world Jerusalem had no river. Babylon rose beside the mighty Euphrates, the cities of Egypt gathered round the majestic fertility of the Nile, Rome was to rise by the Tiber, as London around the Thames, but Jerusalem had no river – only the meagre mercy of one perennial rivulet, 'cool Siloam's shady rill'. River there was none. But there was in the psalmist's eye. It was the same river as Isaiah saw flowing. 'Look upon Zion, city of our solemn feasts, let your eyes rest on Jerusalem . . . it will be a place of rivers and broad streams.' It was the same river as Ezekiel saw welling up from the Temple and growing in size and power until it reached the Dead Sea, and even those poisonous waters became sweet and life-sustaining. It was perhaps the river that you find in Genesis, 'A river flowed out of Eden to water the garden . . .'

In other words this is a river that was marked on no map, as the city was reared at no geographical point. It is perhaps worth noting that in the NEB there is a footnote appended to the phrase 'the city of God'. It reads 'or, a wondrous city'. It *is* the city of God that is being described, but not Jerusalem (save in so far as there was the yearning that Jerusalem would more and more become '*Blessed* City, *heavenly* Salem'). It is 'the Golden City' – the city in which men of faith have found that God makes his dwelling and his throne with the pure in heart does not mean the perfect, but it does mean the committed, the men and women who in their frailty have still tried to commit themselves to the ways of God. It is not a city in the sense of a collection of build-ings, but in the sense of a *community*, men and women bound together by their commitment to God.

In that community the river symbolizes God's sustaining and refreshing ministry. You see the superb contrast? The poem begins with the roar and clash of mighty destructive waters . . .

then suddenly, 'Lo, a river whose streams refresh the city of God.' How impressive the water-spouts and cataracts, how awe-inspiring the seas that engulf the mountains, how totally mind-bending the sheer destructive force of the powers of chaos and evil! How gentle the river, how almost secret and imperceptible the flow of its divided streams, how tiny as it becomes divided up into a myriad rivulets flowing into individual lives! But—cries the psalmist, in effect—it is the ordered quiet, the calm flow of God's peace, God's power, God's very self into human lives which is the *really* impressive thing, the eternal and indestructible thing. 'After the earthquake the still small voice.' This is the psalm which closes with the words, 'Be still, and know that I am God.' It does not mean 'Meditate on God', but it does mean among other things, 'Let go, let go of your scurrying around and frantic activity, and your panic and your vulnerability that makes you so easily dominated by all that is noisy and outwardly impressive, and just see me at work.' Rest, shelter if you like, in the thought of the *quiet* operation of God, whose river produces no noisy crash of billows but steadily flows to cleanse, irrigate and quicken true human life.

It is that stream the psalmist sees that also supplies the moat which garrisons the heart that finds in God a high stronghold. The man who knows God's activity in this way is sheltered from despair, be the earth never so unquiet. His confidence has a secret; his life has an underground river, if you like, which gives to the besieged a power to hold out when faith is assailed. There is no promise to the man of faith that he will be sheltered from life's testing times. He may be the more sensitive to the world's miseries because he is a man of faith. What is promised is that God is a high stronghold, and there is a river whose streams gladden the hearts of God's community. That shelter we *are* offered, and we should seek no other.

Refrains to hymns are 'out' in cultured circles today. They smack too much of Moody and Sankey and a rousing emotionalism much to be deprecated. But the psalmists were not so fastidious. Refrains were widely used, and this glorious psalm – 107 – has a splendid one. In the familiar A V it goes 'Oh, that men would praise the Lord for his goodness, and for his wonderful works to the children of men.' The first thirty-two verses constitute the real psalm, and the remainder of the verses a later edition by another hand. The original psalm is a hymn that was sung in the Temple courts when pilgrims have been 'gathered out of every land, from east and west, from north and south', as an early verse puts it. It is a hymn with four verses, sung perhaps by four different groups, with everybody joining in the chorus. The chorus runs in the NEB:

> Let them thank the LORD for his enduring love
> and for the marvellous things he has done for men.

We can picture the refrain being sung by the two sides of the crowd in the Temple. One company would sing:

> Let them thank the LORD for his enduring love

and the other would crash back with the response –

> and for the marvellous things he has done for men.

And who are the people who are being summoned to thanksgiving? The four groups who are described in the four different verses of the hymn.

Picture the scene. The first verse is sung by the travellers, the pilgrims who have made a long, arduous journey to come to the Temple, and a journey that has awakened ancestral memories of how God had made himself known on a journey that all the children of Israel had made as they tramped through the wilderness after they left slavery in Egypt.

Some lost their way in desert wastes;
    they found no road to a city to live in;
  hungry and thirsty,
    their spirit sank within them.

Each of the verses of the hymn begins like that with some grim plight that men had known, and the desperation to which it brought them, and a sense that human resources were bankrupt.

So they cried to the Lord in their trouble,
    and he saved them from their distress.

And each time the salvation is in the specific form they need – in this case 'he led them by a straight and easy way, until they came to a city to live in'. And then comes the refrain.

Now another group takes up the next verse. Their faces are pale – they are men who have known imprisonment. Sometimes it was an actual imprisonment for punishment, sometimes a sense that life had shut them in and denied them freedom. Most felt that their own wrongdoing had done that.

Some sat in darkness, dark as death,
    prisoners bound fast in iron,
  because they had rebelled against God's commands
    and flouted the purpose of the Most High.

In that last phrase we get the freshness of our new translation. The A V uses a phrase which has not the slightest impact on our minds today: 'and contemned the counsel of the Most High'. No one alive today ever heard anyone say 'You've contemned my orders', but 'flouted' is a living and strong word; 'They flouted every rule in the book.'

They, too, cry to God, and he delivers them. The same rhythm of a grim plight, a human despair, a turning to God, and the answer that the need, in this instance deliverance, a breaking of chains.

Again the refrain crashes out. And then there comes another verse, and this time the voices that raise it seem weak and wavery, the voices of men only convalescent. In Old Testament days they thought of illness as punishment for wrongdoing, even if unconscious; it added an extra dimension of suffering to the illness itself. We can leave that on one side. This is the verse of men who have known what sickness really was. How much more telling is one phrase that describes the weariness of illness! The AV has it as '. . . Their soul abhorreth all manner of meat'; it makes them sound like rather pompous and old-fashioned vegetarians. The NEB catches the reality of being 'off your food' exactly: it runs, 'They sickened at the sight of food.' And they too cry to God, and 'he sent his word to heal them and bring them alive out of the pit of death'.

Again the refrain crashes out—

> Let them thank the Lord for his enduring love
> and for the marvellous things he has done for men.

And we come to the fourth and last verse of the hymn. This time the men who sing it are not pale with imprisonment, or wasted by sickness. They are ruddy with the wind and the rain; they have eyes looking out to wide horizons and crinkled with being narrowed as the spray came over the ship. For these are the sailors:

> Others there are who go to sea in ships
> and make their living on the wide waters.

But they, too, had known a day of crisis, when the storm blew and the ship was thrown about like a cockle shell:

> Carried up to heaven, plunged down to the depths,
> tossed to and fro in peril,
> they reeled and staggered like drunken men,
> and their seamanship was all in vain.

That last phrase spells out the AV's 'and are at their wits' end'. The skills of seamanship had run out. Man's extremity again, and again God's opportunity. So 'they cried unto the Lord in their trouble, and he brought them out of their distress'. Calm comes 'as he guided them to the harbour they desired'.

And for the last time the great refrain rings out through the Temple courts . . .

> Let them thank the Lord for his enduring love
> and for the marvellous things he has done for men.

It is a grand, a glorious hymn, and it has only one theme. It is 'God's enduring love'. The psalm begins in our NEB version,

> It is good to give thanks to the LORD
> for his love endures for ever.

It may have been a solo voice that sang out the one theme of this great act of praise–and the whole company replied,

> So let them say who were redeemed by the LORD.

Then come the four different concrete experiences of redemption –the travellers who had lost their way in the wilderness, the men imprisoned by their own guilt, the men who had sickened at the sight of food and drawn near to death itself, and the men whose skill had run out in a day of natural disaster. And the great refrain declares that though their original crises were different and contrasted their common supreme experience was of the enduring love of God.

More light comes from our new translation in regard to this central theme than anywhere else in this psalm. The AV hides the theme in a sense by beginning with 'for his mercy endureth for ever' and then in the refrain turning to 'goodness'. Most of all, neither 'mercy' nor 'goodness' is anything like strong enough for the Hebrew word 'Hesed'. The attempt to use only one English word for one Hebrew word will not do. The RSV saw that and called it 'steadfast love': the Jerusalem Bible tried to get away with one word, and used the word 'love', but, alas, that is a word that has become somewhat weakened. Unadorned it does not give the full flavour of the Hebrew, which is what is expressed in the arresting first line of George Matheson's so deeply personal hymn, 'O Love that wilt not let me go'.

This psalm is a hymn sung by men who have realized that

God was with them in every experience of life, and that again and again when their own resources ran out – when they were lost or broken and depressed by moral failure, or sick of body and soul, or in danger when human skill was inadequate – they were delivered. The love of God was strong and steadfast; it *endured*. It therefore demanded this praise and thanksgiving.

4 A God Both Active and Constant
Psalm 145

It is easy to see why psalm 145 has had a close association in Christian worship with Pentecost, Whit Sunday. In Acts you get that marvellous roll-call of where all the people had come from to be there in Jerusalem (for the harvest festival, for that is what Pentecost was in the Hebrew calendar), the 'Parthians and Medes and Elamites', and all the rest. And they are all making one common response: 'We do hear them speak in our own tongues the wonderful works of God'.

'The wonderful works of God'; psalm 145 has no other theme than that. In the NEB verse 5 starts:

> My theme shall be thy marvellous works.

And phrases like that recur right through the psalm.

> One generation shall commend thy works to another
> and set forth thy mighty deeds . . .

> Men shall declare thy mighty acts with awe
> and tell of thy great deeds.

and later:

> they proclaim to their fellows how mighty are thy deeds.

This psalm is in fact an ecstatic hymn of praise to a God mightily at work, and constant in his caring. Among the many fascinating discoveries in those scrolls found in the caves at

Qumran, above the Dead Sea, is a version of this psalm, and after every verse in it is written this refrain:

> Blessed be the Lord, and blessed be his name for ever and ever.

That discovery tells us how this psalm was used. Perhaps one singer, perhaps a group of singers, would sing the verse that sets out some aspect of the wonderful works of God, and then the whole congregation would roar out its refrain and response: 'Blessed be the Lord, and blessed be his name for ever and ever!'

If this hymn is that kind of ecstatic act of praise we can see again how easily it would be taken over by the Christian community for Pentecost. However you interpret that Pentecostal gift of tongues there is a strong element of ecstasy about it, of being caught up in an experience far bigger than themselves and far beyond their normal experience. At Pentecost Christ's followers were overwhelmed with the sense of the greatness of God, of what he had done in Christ and how he had now poured his power into them. And if they had ransacked the whole of scripture they could not have found any part that hymned the greatness of God with greater fervour than this. One commentator remarks that 'nowhere else is there such a piling up of phrases descriptive of the greatness of the Lord'.

Now, just because of this, this is not a psalm that follows a very clear pattern despite its acrostic form. Ecstasy and order are rarely found together. More likely you will find certain themes or ideas recurring again and again. So it is here. We take three of them.

The first is that believing men have a duty, and a joy, to *tell* the greatness of God and his wonderful works, that is, what he has done.

This is certainly a theme that keeps recurring. The AV reads in verse 4, 'One generation shall praise thy works to another, and shall declare thy mighty acts.' The NEB is perhaps a little clearer about the task in hand: 'One generation shall commend thy works to another, and set forth thy mighty deeds.' But it is the same job—and to praise is, I suppose, to declare. When a housewife says 'I've never found anything better for getting out stains than so-and-so', she is both praising it and making a declaration. She is 'setting forth' what it will do.

A couple of verses later the same thought is put into slightly different words. 'Men shall declare thy mighty acts with awe, and tell of thy great deeds.' Here a slight change which the NEB makes clarifies something of immense importance. Where the AV reads 'I will declare thy greatness' the NEB reads 'and tell of thy great deeds'. This reinforces something that is in any case set out again and again elsewhere: the dominant thought is not that of God's greatness just as a quality that belongs to him, but of the great things that God has done.

We might say of Everest, 'That is a supremely great mountain.' To climb it is a feat worthy of record, record throughout the world, just because it is supremely great. There is no other mountain so high. This is a quality that belongs to Everest. But if we say of Winston Churchill that he was the supremely great figure of his generation we are saying something very different. His greatness showed itself in what he did – his power to enthuse a nation in a day of disaster, his leadership, his determination, his strategic thinking and all the rest. Of course, these actions arose from qualities within the man. But his greatness was not a static greatness; it was a dynamic greatness; it showed itself in action. Everest's greatness is a static greatness; you can do things to it– you can climb it and thus explore its greatness. It cannot do things to you.

Now it is possible to talk of God as if the greatness we ascribe to him was something static, like that of Everest. The Bible in all its parts contradicts that. What the Bible says is that the greatness of God is dynamic; it shows itself in his mighty acts, in his marvellous works.

And this implies something – that they must be told. The same theme appears in verses 11 and 12.

> They talk of the glory of thy kingdom
>   and tell of thy might,

> they proclaim to their fellows how mighty are thy deeds,
> how glorious the majesty of thy kingdom.   (NEB)

This note of 'telling' is something quite special about biblical religion, because right through it runs this thought of the great things that God has *done*. The Old Testament rings out with the story of how God saved his people from bondage in Egypt and brought them through all the perils of the wilderness to the promised land. This was the glorious story of God's wonderful acts, and quite literally one generation had to commend God's works to another. It was something that had happened. It was the ground of their confidence in God, and the next generation had to be told about it.

Now clearly this is true of the far greater saving acts of God in history that Whitsuntide began to tell, how a child was born, and how in Galilee and Judea a life was lived, and outside Jerusalem a death was died, and how the One who died was found to be still alive. These are events, events in which God was wonderfully at work, in particular places and at particular times. And if events are to be known they have to be told.

This sheds light on the continuing task of the Christian church. If our faith rested on an idea then ideas can come up again and again in human history; but since it rests on an event, then proclamation, declaration, 'telling', is at the very heart of the task of the Christian church. What began that first Whitsuntide must go on. We must tell the wonderful works of God. We have a special duty to commend the works of God from one generation to the next. Christian nurture of our children belongs to the actual character of the faith that is ours in a God whose greatness is shown in what he has done.

Another recurrent theme is that these wonderful works are the works of a caring, loving God. Once again the NEB gives us a stronger reading. Where the AV says that God is 'of great mercy', the NEB says he is 'constant in his love'.

Mercy to us today suggests being let off the consequences of our misdeeds. So a merciful judge is one who tempers the strict demands of justice with kindness. But the thought of God as constant in his love is far wider; it sweeps right across the whole of life. And so does this psalm in illustration of it, from verse 14 right on.

Verse 14 is of quite particular interest, for here in the first two lines the NEB gives us words that were just not there in the older translation of our Bible. 'How dare the new translators add to our Bible?' you may ask. What they have done is to recover a most precious verse that had become lost.

In fact this psalm is an acrostic. In Hebrew poetry an acrostic was a poem with verses which began with a letter of the alphabet, all in the right order, so that when you looked down the first letters of the verses of the whole poem you saw the whole alphabet . . . aleph, beth, ghimel . . . right on. But in the Hebrew text that has come down to us the verse that should begin with 'Nun' is missing. You can tell there is something missing from the gap in the alphabet. In the Greek version of the Old Testament, called the Septuagint, and in ancient versions in other languages it is there. So the NEB has put it back into place, and translated it. Here it is:

> In all his promises the LORD keeps faith,
> he is unchanging in all his works.

This was worth recovering. It spells out what that phrase 'constant in his love' means. Here is a God who always performs what he promises, and whose actions have about them an unchanging consistency.

You cannot always say that even about the actions of a great man. The very man who is immensely active, dynamic, powerful in his deeds is often the man who, if not erratic, has still an occasional glaring inconsistency. Just because of his greatness, just because of the power that is behind his actions, there is about such wayward inconsistency a terrible character. It is very striking in the life of Martin Luther. Here was a man who did tremendous things for living religion, a great man colossally active in reforming the church. But when he made errors, as in

encouraging the princes to crush the Peasants' Revolt with ruth-
less severity, they were appalling errors. The vehement force of
his personality gave them a terrible power.

But, it might be said, God is God and man is man. You can
expect man to be erratic at times, but is it not just a platitude to
say that God is consistent? It was not in the ancient world. Read
the Greek stories about the gods and the one thing you could say
they had in common was that they were unpredictable. Nor is it
only in the ancient world that you find such notions: they survive
to the present day. How much popular religion and superstition
rest on ideas of the unpredictability of God or fate!

The glory of Hebrew religion, as we see it in this psalm, was
that it portrayed a God who was mighty in his acts and constant
in his love at the same time. As the rest of verse 14 goes on:

> the LORD upholds up those who stumble
> and straightens backs which are bent.

(This is clearer than the AV's 'The Lord upholdeth all who fall,
and raiseth up all those that he bowed down.' It is when we
stumble that we need the hand put out to steady us, and when
things are getting us down–when our backs are bent–that we
need straightening.)

This psalm further brings together two great notes which are
sounded in the Whitsuntide message. They are the notes of the
intimate and the universal, God as near and God as everywhere.

One little word runs through this psalm, the word 'all'. 'The
Lord is good to all men,' 'His tender care rests upon all his
creatures,' 'All thy creatures praise thee,' 'thy dominion stands
for all generations,' 'The eyes of all are lifted to thee in hope,'
'The Lord watches over all who love him,' 'all creatures shall
bless his holy name.'

But there is also a wonderful verse–refreshingly clear in our
new translation–'very near is the Lord to those who call to him'
(v. 18 NEB). God is everywhere, his caring hand is upon all
living things, but 'very near is the Lord to those who call to him'.

This was fulfilled at Pentecost. Here is the pouring out of

God's spirit upon all flesh, the spirit thus given is to go out smashing down every barrier between men, just as the curse of Babel was miraculously lifted so that all who were there heard the wonderful works of God in their own language. But what is universal is also very intimate and particular. The gift of the Spirit is the assurance that 'very near is the Lord to those who call to him'; he is the picture of God indwelling.

4

Songs out of the Depths

1   A Cry of Anguish
Psalm 38

'Lord, don't be angry and rebuke me! Don't punish me in your anger! You have punished me and wounded me; you have struck me down' (TEV). How freshly, how sharply the anguish comes through in the words of our ordinary speech compared with the mellow and stately cadences of 'O Lord, rebuke me not in thy wrath: neither chasten me in thy hot displeasure'–though even there the one adjective 'hot' reflects the rawness of the emotion.

The psalter was a hymnbook, the hymnbook of the Temple, so even this poem torn from the bleeding heart of an individual became used by many voices. They were not as fastidious as the compilers of at least one major hymnbook who consign the more deeply personal hymns like 'There is a fountain filled with blood' and 'O Love that wilt not let me go' to a section fenced off with the title 'Chiefly for Private Devotion'. In fact the scholars who have been exploring in our century the use of the psalter in the liturgy and worship of the Jewish people tell us that this intensely personal psalm, this cry of anguish from a pierced and battered man, was used as a kind of prayer of intercession for any grievously sick person. At first glance that looks strange. Many concerned with Christian healing would have asked us rather to lift up such a person into that realm of wholeness and serenity from which healing could come. Does this mean, then, that such a notion as using this anguished psalm as a prayer for healing is lamentably sub-Christian? No, for its function would be to encourage that entering into the actual situation of pain and misery of the sufferer with as deep a compassion as possible which makes intercession a reality for us. We do not really intercede for anybody unless there is some attempt imaginatively and sensitively to get inside their skins and their situation. If this psalm's words were really listened to by the singers there in the Temple courts they would have been remembering a real man in an actual situation when they prayed for anyone through the medium of it.

For though that may have been the use of the psalm, and how it therefore came to be handed down to us, it is certainly not its origin. No man sat down and composed this psalm for worship. This is the kind of thing that is torn out of a man, or that surges out of him because he believes that even by giving his anguish expression it may be in some degree lessened and abated. In the inelegant phrase of today, this is a 'gut reaction', not an intellectual exercise.

Does it nonetheless seem rather exaggerated?

> Because I have been foolish, my sores stink and rot:
> I am bent over, I am crushed; I mourn all day long.
> I am burning with fever, and I am seriously ill.
> I am utterly crushed and defeated; my heart is troubled,
> and I groan with pain. (TEV)

Does all that is English in us wriggle and murmur, 'Not very manly, old chap, what about consuming your own smoke, eh? Never heard of the stiff upper lip?' And, of course, part of the answer is that he had not, and that the public school ethic even came in long after Dr Arnold's day at Rugby. Read around the mid-Victorian period and it is amazing how emotional they all were. Men burst into tears and are unable to control their emotions. And since the psalmist had not had the inestimable benefit of being an upper-class Englishman influenced by Rudyard Kipling ('You'll be a man, my son'), he just had to struggle on as best he might.

But, more seriously, we feel perhaps that as well as giving very open expression to his emotions he is exaggerating them, even wallowing in them. There are passages in the book of Job that are very like this, though nowhere does Job link his suffering to his sin. I recall a story about the young B. K. Cunningham, who was later to be one of the greatest teachers of priests the Church of England has ever known. When he was a young man in his twenties serving in Delhi and offering to read to an older, very sick colleague from the Bible, the patient chose a passage from Job and 'BK' began to read: 'Let the day perish wherein I was born, and the night in which it was said, There is a man child conceived.' He stopped and looked at the patient who lay peacefully, however, with his eyes closed. 'BK' plunged on: 'Why died I not from the womb? Why did I not give up the ghost when I came out of the belly?' 'Beautiful, beautiful,' murmured the sick man. 'BK' felt he had to persevere. 'Wherefore is light given to him that is in misery and life unto the bitter in soul; which long for death, but it cometh not?' Then he stopped and said, 'I say, old fellow, do you *really* feel as bad as that?' 'Yes, indeed, Cunningham,' he replied earnestly, 'I know that I am going to die and I am sure that I shall go to hell.' 'BK' wondered what to say, and at last just said, 'What'll you bet?' The patient was so startled and cheered that he was living fifty years later.

'What'll you bet?' That cheerful derisive phrase seems to express a good deal of what we feel about all this exaggerated oriental emotion. But there is another side to this. Alexander Maclaren refers to an 'Eastern vehemence in utterance of emotions which Western reticence prefers to let gnaw in silence at the roots of life.' Is it a good thing for suppressed and repressed emotion to gnaw at the roots of life? I wonder what the relative incidence of mental and nervous breakdown is as between the Orient and the 'stiff upper lip' land of our birth. Is it always wise to bottle up our agony? I wonder how many of us could put our hand on our heart and swear when we were going through some bad patch of physical pain, earache or something of the kind, that there were not times when we were on our own that we did just what the psalmist did, 'Groaned with pain', yes, and found it helped?

One of the great glories of the psalms is that again and again the psalmist dares to say what we would like to say and feel bound by reticence or a pretence to orthodoxy to refrain from saying. Thank heaven and again and again the psalmist is a bit of a bounder. He actually says what goes on in his heart, or shouts at God for being so long in giving the wicked their deserts, or so slow at coming to the rescue of the godly. Sometimes the psalmist shouts in faith and hope, constantly he shouts in praise, and now and then–as in our psalm–he just shouts that it is hurting. He is in pain, it is awful, he does not know what to do, he does not know which way to turn, it is driving him mad.

It is one of the secrets of the endurance of the psalms that this is true. They dare to give expression to what men actually feel, not the pretences they put up in polite society. Here is what a man actually felt like, what he spilled out on to his parchment because it was just like that.

There is another barrier between this man and us today to be tackled before we go any further. It is that he identifies his suffering as God's punishment for his sin. Now it would be absurd to deny that some suffering and disease are the plain consequence of wrong-doing. But we have emerged from such a total identification, and we have Jesus' own warrant for doing so. But that was that man's situation, and it grievously accentuated his problem and his consequent anguish.

At least three helpful things emerge from this, at first glance, unpromising psalm.

One is that even if a man cannot argue he can cry out in his need. Mark the contrast here between this psalmist and the man portrayed in the immediately preceding book of the Bible–Job. Job, too, has an appalling problem of suffering, but Job is an articulate man, an intellectual man. Job is a man who can argue, argue with his friends who pose as comforters but are only aggravators of his anguish, yes, and argue with God, too. If you read that drama there are moments when you feel that the agony of Job must even in a measure have been assuaged by the power he had of putting his massive argument into words. 'And Job answered and said, "No doubt but ye are the people, and wisdom shall die with you. But I have understanding as well as you; I am not inferior to you: yea, who knoweth not such things as these?" ' To possess such reserves of scorn and irony and pithy compelling sentences must itself have brought something of comfort.

But while our psalmist is vocal in the sense that he emphatically does not bottle things up, he is not articulate in the sense of Job. Intellectually he cannot grapple with what is happening to him. He groans and moans and falls (as we do at such points) into the repetitiveness of self-pity. He can say what is happening, but he cannot cope with it, reason his way through it. He can only let out the cry of a trapped creature.

And one thing this psalm says to us is, 'Shout out to God, shout out to him about what you feel but do not understand. Do not be ashamed of not being able to reason things through. Do not be ashamed that to feel as you do suggests that you haven't much faith, much spirituality in you. Say, "Father, this is what it feels like, and it is hell, and I want help, and I want it now." '

Again, the psalmist may feel that it is because of his sin that he is suffering as he is, he may be making the cruel identification of his time of suffering with sin, he may feel that his anguish has its root in God's anger – but he still believes that God cares and God will listen. His pain is gravely aggravated by the attitude of others to him.

> My friends and my companions shun me in my sickness,
> and my kinsfolk keep far away.

A consequence of the theory that suffering was punishment for sin was that even friends and relations tended to shun the sufferer because he must be a sinner. Nor did modern theories of infection and contagion need to be worked out for a general notion to be abroad that you might catch something if you went near to the sick man. But apart from all that, how many have found that in

the time of their bitterest distress – time of breakdown or whatever it might be – a sense of alienation from those previously dear
is a vile part of the experience?

If that was the behaviour of friends, what could be expected of
enemies?

> Those who wish me dead defame me,
> those who mean to injure me spread cruel gossip
> and mutter slanders all day long.   (NEB)

I wonder if they in fact did? Isn't this part of the neurotic effect
of suffering? It is part of that grim process of alienation in which
the sufferer feels cut off from human contact and sympathy. There
is a telling verse where he says, 'I am like a deaf man, and cannot
hear, like a dumb man, and cannot speak, I am like a man who
does not answer, because he cannot hear.'

What a vivid portrayal that is, coming from that ancient time,
of this tragic sense of being cut off from meaningful human
contact, from the ability to communicate with those who are not
passing through the same experience.

It is against this black background that the fact stands out that
he still has a sense of God's care, a sense that he can still cry to God
and be heard. 'On thee, O Lord, I fix my hope; thou wilt answer,
O Lord my God.' And the very closing verse is just such a cry.
Listen to it as the Jerusalem Bible gives it:

> Yahweh, do not desert me,
> do not stand aside, my God!
> Come quickly to my help,
> Lord, my saviour!

We may dislike the rendering in that translation of the name of
God as Yahweh, but here it has real justification, for only this
translation reveals a striking fact. It is that the psalmist in this last
cry calls God by all three names by which he was known, as
Jehovah or Yahweh, Adonai and Elohim. 'Yahweh', 'my God',
'Lord', all three come. This is not a point about language, about
ancient nomenclature for God. It is a point about the human
heart. The anguish of that cry for help, and the element of doubt

mixed up in his faith, are revealed by the determination to call on God by every name by which he is known. If he does not hear and respond to the one he might to the other.

For let us not pretend. There is no certainty in this cry; it still has in it the element of desperation. And let us not take the easy way out and say, 'Ah, but this was written before men came to know God in Christ. Today we can be far more certain.' Perhaps we can be, and certainly we have greater ground for our faith, and through the cross a deeper insight as to how God can use all suffering. But when all is said and done, this poor man's cry still stays true for many of us. We can be glad that there is still some sense of the channel of communication being open between God and ourselves, even if all we can send along it be a shout of anguish. We can be glad that the scriptures of our faith contain not just men's certainties but men's gropings and men's cries. The honesty and the lack of reticence of this man's cry speak for us, and we are grateful.

2 A Cry for Deliverance
Psalm 40

There is something odd about a psalm that begins with the firm statement, 'I waited, waited for the Lord, he bent down to me and heard my cry . . .' and ends with the anguished cry 'O my God, make no delay.' There seems, to put no finer point upon it, to be some inconsistency here, for one cry is a shout of confidence and the other is almost a shriek of desperation.

So odd does it seem to be that when the fact is added that the closing verses of this psalm reappear in scarcely altered form in psalm 70 many scholars have come to the conclusion that the fortieth psalm is an arbitrary joining together of disparate things. It does not really all belong together is this argument, and the verses from twelve onwards, beginning

> For misfortunes beyond counting
> press on me from all sides . . .

right on to the broken cry for speedy help from God have become accidentally attached to the earlier verses.

But can we be sure? One or two of the more recent commentators have firmly questioned this cutting of the psalm into unrelated pieces. Earlier scholars may have been informed about literary problems and textual issues, but had they concentrated enough on what human beings are really like?

There are people that are spoken of as manic-depressives. The description makes it a grim state of mind, and certainly it can become a tragic one. But some of the writers and artists and thinkers who have greatly enriched life come under that description. And many of us, without being so marked in our emotional see-sawing as to be so described, have an element of this in our make-up. The manic-depressive violently see-saws between ecstatic happiness and confidence and dark depression and nervous fears. It is a state that should earn our deep sympathy, and a sympathy not hard to give because there is enough of an element of this in the make-up of most of us to give us an inbuilt sympathy.

More than that, it is a commonplace in the lives of the saints that the very people who can spiritually soar to the seventh heaven are those who have to face that terrible malady often called 'the dark night of the soul'. Without belonging to those rare mystical souls we all know a fearful gap between the spiritual insight and warmth of a Sunday and the ordinary misery of a wet Monday morning waiting for the 'bus on a windy corner.

None of us is consistent, and none of us is set in unchanging circumstances. 'Are there any deliverances in this perilous and incomplete life so entire and permanent that they leave no room for further perils?' (Maclaren).

If we put the scissors aside that would cut up the psalm according to consistency of mood, we can thank God that his psalmist is inconsistent, that his moods and his experiences are like ours, a very mixed bag. This singer in Israel sang an inconsistent song, part of it lyrical in thanksgiving and part of it discordant in its plaintiveness. He was, if you like, manic-depressive. There is abandonment of that godly pretence which (if we are honest) can at times deeply depress us. The godly pretence is that when God has given us a victory we are for ever at peace, at least on that front. It is not true. It was not true for Jesus himself. John Huxtable has discerningly said, 'In Gethsemane our Lord refought the battle of which his earthly life was chiefly composed.' In Gethsemane at the last Jesus had to face the temptations which had met him across Jordan. God had to give his victory over and over again. If that was true of Jesus, it is likely to be very true for us.

Throughout our studies we have seen that the book of psalms is richly, and even disturbingly, human. The parts of the psalms that perturb us are richly human – the blatant hatred of enemies, the cruel wish that the enemies of God and of the psalmist (and they are often identical in the writer's view) should suffer punishment, the girding at God, the smug satisfaction. A great deal is naturally sub-Christian. But the psalter is valuably made up of the songs of men as they really are, not as ideally they might be, and it is about life as it in fact is and not life as we wish it were.

We look then at this 40th psalm as a unity and particularly those parts of it which are most open to the charge of inconsistency.

It begins with a song of thanksgiving for deliverance.

> he set my feet on a rock
> and gave me a firm footing;
> and on my lips he put a new song,
> a song of praise to our God. (NEB)

Even here there is a note of realism. The old version has the opening words, 'I waited patiently for the Lord,' but the new one is even more true to the Hebrew when it goes, 'I waited, waited for the Lord.' We say, 'I waited and waited for the 'bus – and it never came.' This is the force of that double 'waited' in the NEB, and it reproduces the original very accurately. The end of the quotation is different from the 'bus. God acted. But the wait called for an equal patience. The psalmist does not encourage us to believe that God's action in crisis will come as speedily as we want it.

It was indeed crisis that the psalmist was undergoing. He says that he was in a muddy pit, in the mire and the clay. In the Near East in the ancient world these pictures were very customary images for the underworld, the place of death. It may be that the psalmist refers to some ghastly accident or dire illness that causes him almost to slip into the realm of the dead, as they then pictured it. It may be a more spiritual illness of which he speaks so graphically. Certainly those vivid pictures would represent for most of us all too accurate a representation of what it feels like when for some reason the ground gives way beneath our feet and we are sliding and slithering about without any firm foothold anywhere and on anything. Life has become a nightmare from which there is no blissful waking because we *are* awake, and it is real. The facts are there; the person we loved most is dead, we have failed to get that longed-for job or opportunity, we are facing this or that enmity and harshness from people, we have made a mess of life in this or that way. The nightmare is real, it is daytime actuality. We are in the miry pit, on the slithery clay.

And what the psalmist had found was that there was a rock jutting out into the middle of the marshy ground. What power could lift him from the yielding bog to the firm foothold? Only one, God. He waited, waited for the Lord—crying to him, and God bent down and lifted him out and set his foot upon the rock. How exactly it had happened he perhaps could never have factually described; that it *had* happened no man more gloriously knew. When but a little while before all life's foundations had gone now his feet were walking on firm ground, and he sang a new song. He begins this song with that new song, he begins it with the experience of deliverance. This is where all prayer should begin, with what God has done.

But if this psalm is a unity he does not end his song there, or when he has worked out the wider implications of his experience for the company of the faithful. He has honestly to confess that he needs another victory.

> For misfortunes beyond counting
> press on me from all sides;
> my iniquities have overtaken me,
> and my sight fails;
> they are more than the hairs of my head,
> and my courage forsakes me.

It is easy to say, 'Where is the man's faith that he was boasting of a moment ago? Does his new song of deliverance get drowned in this moaning as quickly as this?' But this is how human beings do feel and act.

In fact the point of great spiritual experience is very often the point of great danger. Negative forces move in at the point of reaction, and the nervous systems of most of us react after great experiences. Elijah cracked when he had had the great victory over the prophets of Baal on Mount Carmel and ran away before Jezebel's threat, muttering away about being the only faithful person in Israel and now his life was in danger. He had just won, but he felt defeated. Or, on a more whimsical note, there is the remark of a wry sort attributed to T. R. Glover, the author of *The Jesus of History*, who was one of the most inspiring speakers ever to address the great gatherings of students who used to come together at the Swanwick Conference Centre in Derbyshire. 'How often I have left Swanwick uplifted,' he used to say, 'only for the devil and all his angels to meet me on Derby Midland Station.'

It is the way it happened for the writer of our psalm. Everything seemed to go wrong at once – 'misfortunes beyond counting press on me from all sides'. Nor was it only outward events; there comes the consciousness of inward failure. When life starts going wrong outwardly it starts going wrong inwardly, too. Or at least our nervous system so works that when events bring us low there rush into our memories all the embarrassing and foolish and wrong things that we have done in the past.

Then *your sight fails*! That is what the psalmist says, and he is right. Your spiritual vision goes, and with your vision goes your courage. 'And my courage forsakes me.'

But the wonder of the ending of that psalm is no poorer than that of its glorious beginning about the deliverance from the miry pit and the new song of praise set upon his lips. For out of that 'dark night of the soul' that has just been described the cry of urgent faith arises:

> Show me favour, O LORD, and save me;
> hasten to help me, O LORD.
>
> . . . I am poor and needy;
> O LORD, think of me.
> Thou art my help and salvation;
>   O my God, make no delay.

He is again waiting, waiting. He is making no pretences. He is poor in spirit. He is not spiritually tough. He has no rich stores of spiritual strength to draw upon in a day like this when evil batters him. If there is to be any deliverance for him, it is God who has to give it. And he cannot pretend either that he can hold out much longer. He is like a man whose foot has slipped and he is hanging out over space by aching fingers with strength ebbing. 'O my God, make no delay.'

We cannot minimize a faith like that; it is as real as a man's flesh and blood. He looked back and he remembered that God had once delivered him. But once was not enough, and it is not enough for us either. 'Our Pharaohs are seldom drowned in the Red Sea, and we do not often see their corpses stretched on the sand' (Maclaren). They still pursue hard after us, and we need God's help and we need it fast. It is not a failure of faith to cry out for such speedy help; it is the very act of a living faith. It says in effect, 'O God who has delivered me in the past deliver me now by the same power, for I am just about to fall.'

> O LORD, think of me.
> Thou art my help and salvation;
>   O my God, make no delay.

5

Songs on Pilgrimage

1   Joy in Journeying
Psalm 84

Robert Louis Stevenson wrote 'To travel hopefully is a better thing than to arrive.' They are words usually admired, suggesting the carefree spirit of swinging along the road with knapsack on your back, with 'the wind on the heath' in George Borrow fashion, invigorated by the challenge of the obstacles on the path and captivated by the promise of the golden city over the horizon. Maybe, but if you look at the words they are curiously cynical; they suggest that the gold of the golden city may only be gold paint. If to travel hopefully is in fact better than to arrive then the hopes are dupes: you have been 'had'. You may enjoy the journey, travelling along hopefully, but when you get there you find it has all been a 'con'. The journey with your illusions is better than arrival with its disillusionment.

So if the object of faith be a disappointment when it is reached and experienced, if the substance of our hopes be found to be insubstantial when we arrive, then we have been exploited.

But with this said with some emphasis, it can also be said that there is a particular and real joy in pilgrimage, an experience that you have when you are on the road, rather than arriving, which is its own authentic part of our knowledge of God and his goodness to us.

This is one of the big things that psalm 84 is saying. The whole psalm is one of pilgrimage, possibly (as some think) written by a man who travelled from his home in a pagan country to the centre of his ancestral faith at the Temple in Jerusalem. It is possibly associated with the great autumnal festival, and in any case set on the lips of people who had journeyed to be there at worship. It is possibly a psalm of entrance, that is, one sung just as the pilgrims coming up for the festival were reaching the goal of their journey and passing into the Temple courts.

One stanza of the poem brings together the being there and the journeying there.

> Happy are those who dwell in thy house;
>   they never cease from praising thee.
> Happy the men whose refuge is in thee,
>   whose hearts are set on the pilgrim ways!
>
> (vv. 4–5 NEB)

The image of the psalmist in picturing God's house as man's home and fulfilment is familiar through Henry Francis Lyte's use of it in his hymn 'Pleasant are thy courts above'.

> Even the sparrow finds a home,
>   and the swallow has her nest,
> where she rears her brood beside thy altars

is the NEB reference to support

> Happy birds that sing and fly
> Round thine altars, O Most High.

The imprecision of academic knowledge of the actualities of Jerusalem life of the period is amusingly illustrated by one scholar telling us that the Temple was thought of as a sanctuary for wild things to which the birds would be welcomed, and another writing of the care with which the Temple buildings were cleansed making it impossible to think of the birds nesting in any part of the sacred structure. The discussion is almost pointless. The poet is using the strongest image there is for home, the nest. (Jesus was to use it negatively about himself.) The psalmist is saying how lovely it is to have your nest in the Temple, the place where men found God more than anywhere else. He thinks of the priests who are there all the time.

> Happy are those who dwell in thy house;
> they never cease from praising thee.

To have arrived, perhaps never to have had to make the journey, to be *there*, nesting there like a bird, praising there like the priests who were, if not in residence, working there through the day, literally at home in God's house . . . how tremendous that must be.

But even as he exclaims like that, another thought comes that in a measure qualifies if it does not contradict it. The thought is how tremendous the experience of pilgrimage has been . . . He expresses it by another benediction with which he follows immediately the one about the happiness of those who are there all the time. The point of this does not appear in the AV: 'Blessed is the man whose strength is in thee; in whose heart are the ways of them.' The last two words are in italics in the AV, which means that there is no Hebrew to support them. They are added to make sense. But what sense do they make? 'In whose heart are the ways of them' – of whom, or of what? What the Hebrew actually says is 'who have highways in their hearts'. And our NEB has in inspired fashion rendered it as: 'whose hearts are set on the pilgrim ways'. What the psalmist is saying is that if the men are happy who are there all the time, who have arrived (if indeed they have ever had to journey), happy, too, are the men whose hearts are set on the pilgrim ways.

His main thought must be what he has learned in the pilgrimage, but there may well be another thought here, too. It is that there is a happiness for the man whose heart is set on the pilgrim ways even if his feet have never been able to be set on them. Nor is this a point only related to days when men thought it necessary to make a physical journey to the object of faith. There are still pilgrimages men may want to make, of which the opportunity is denied. Plain obligation and duty, like care of a growing family or of ageing parents, can hold a man or woman back from some good enterprise which he or she passionately longs to embark upon. The cynic thinks it would have been better had the longing never gripped him; the religious man will think that it makes a difference to our human-ness even if we are condemned to the humdrum when the heart is set on the pilgrim ways.

So this thought is not outdated and irrelevant. There are present-day equivalents of those men of whom the psalmist may compassionately have thought, men who far from dwelling in the Temple, would never even like himself have the chance and thrill of seeing it. Their physical eyes would never rest on that lovely sight, but in their hearts were the pilgrim ways and because of that they would be blessed, even though the tug was at times hard to bear because of the frustration.

But there were things the psalmist believed were to be learned in the actuality of pilgrimage. They had found that the weary, dry and arid experiences of life could know transformation. This is what is being said in the verse which in the AV goes:

> Who passing through the valley of Baca make it a well;
> the rain also filleth the pools.

Where was the valley of Baca? Was it an actual place? Dr Moffatt, with a bold Scotticism, in his translation makes it a place-name calling it 'Weary-glen', the NEB calls it 'the thirsty valley', TEV calls it 'the dry valley', the Jerusalem Bible 'the Valley of the Weeper'. In seven of the extant manuscripts of the psalms, and in what are called 'the versions', i.e. old translations into other oriental languages, it is 'the valley of tears'. Whatever the strictly accurate translation, and whether it is an actual place or not, it seems to stand for the dry and arid place, where the only water that flows is that which emerges from the traveller's eyes as he strives to make his way through this valley that is weary for the pilgrim indeed.

And the psalmist says that the pilgrim spirit can transform it.

> As they pass through the thirsty valley
> they find water from a spring;
> and the LORD provides even men who lose their way
> with pools to quench their thirst.   (NEB)

Again, these are the words of a poet. Dry valleys do not suddenly become filled with refreshing pools in the physical sense because it is pilgrims that are passing through them. (Although we may perhaps read in here the thought that when the pilgrims have got to the Temple for the autumn festival and prayed, as they did, for the life-giving rain, the whole situation would be transformed, so that with the eyes of faith and hope they see the valleys already as they will be when they come through them on their return journey.)

We are not chiefly to interpret what is being said in some woodenly materialistic fashion. They are words written as the poet looks back and sees how happy the man is whose heart is set on the pilgrim ways. What is dry, weary and wearing can be transformed.

Another discovery that was made on the pilgrim way is contained in the verse:

They go from strength to strength, as the AV has it, or as TEV puts it:

> They grow stronger as they go.

Men are kept back from setting out on a real pilgrimage, in the sense of committed discipleship, because they feel that their feeble strength will give out. When things get tough, or when they get further and further away from the impulse that drove them to the commitment, they will get weaker. Circumstances and temptations will get them down. Spiritual energy will desert them, for what they had will be used up.

What the psalmist is saying is that this fear is enervating illusion, to be dismissed as that. Probably he was referring primarily to physical strength on the actual pilgrimage that he and his companions had made. When we are caught up in some really exciting experience we have not got time to be tired. We may 'feel it afterwards' (as we say), but the experience itself carried us on and we did not have time to think how tired we were. It has been like that for the psalmist and his fellow pilgrims; the nearer they got to Zion the more the thought of what lay ahead annihilated their sense of weariness. They grew stronger as they went.

But even the psalmist probably meant what he said more deeply. The inner pilgrimage, too, is not susceptible to the argument that the further you go the more tired you become. Rather for the true disciples it is a matter of 'They grow stronger as they go.' Here we may borrow our illustration from physical walking. A young man spent some three months leading walks of a very demanding sort from a Lakeland mountain-walking centre. Most of the guests were there for a week or a fortnight. He was there for thirteen weeks. In the first weeks the weariness was terrible, day after day, climbing those fells, but in the last month or more he was tireless. Muscles that had screamed for mercy now effortlessly obeyed him; sinews that seemed over-strained were not felt any more; lungs that had ached with up-ward tramping now readily supplied the breath for conquests of the peaks. 'They grow stronger as they go.'

Many a spiritual effort which looks impossible now, can be made as strength builds up on the journey. This is a discovery that could never be made in any other situation. Therefore 'happy the men . . . whose hearts are set on the pilgrim ways'.

Another pilgrim discovery is a fresh scale of values. It is contained in the verse which in the old version reads, 'A day in thy courts is better than a thousand.' It is a curiously inconclusive statement, and readily lends itself to cynical comment. It means, as the NEB gives it:

> Better one day in thy courts
>   than a thousand days at home;
> better to linger by the threshold of God's house
>   than to live in the dwellings of the wicked.

Time is strangely elastic. One day drenched with glorious and happy memories can mean far more to us than a thousand grey routine spans of twenty-four hours. And who would not say that it is better just to have glimpses of some wonderful occasion, even just across the threshold, at the doorway, than to be ensconced in comfort where nothing that matters is going on?

The psalmist is saying that his pilgrimage has made him see this, and to value in a fresh way the opportunity of some living encounter with God. Even to stand on the threshold of the outer court is better than to be at home in pagan comfort. He has been given a new scale of values.

2 Journey to Justice
Psalm 122

There is no piece of church music I love more than the anthem Parry wrote for the Coronation of Edward VII which has been sung at every later coronation. It is a setting of psalm 122. It begins with a quite astonishing shout on three rising notes, 'I was glad, glad when they said unto me, Let us go unto the house of the Lord.' It is sung in procession, symbolizing the pilgrim people of God moving towards the holy place.

Why was the psalmist glad when other people said, 'Let us go unto the house of the Lord'? Because if he had gone on his own he might have been mugged, in today's appropriately ugly word for an ugly phenomenon. There seems a startling contrast between hearing Parry's setting of these words sung in solemn ecclesiastical procession and this down-to-earth fact which caused the original words to be written. But all the commentators agree that he was glad because it just was not safe to travel alone. The lonely traveller was the man those early muggers were looking for, as in a later century they looked for the man about whom Jesus told the story of the Good Samaritan. That victim was on his way home ('a certain man went from Jerusalem to Jericho'), but they were ready for him and they got him, and did just what the violent ruffians do today on the deserted Underground platform, or wherever the traveller might be found alone and vulnerable.

So the poet who wrote this psalm rejoiced that there were

people in his village who said, when festival time came round, 'Come on, let's go up to the Temple, let's go to Jerusalem.' 'I was glad when they said unto me, Let us go unto the House of the Lord.'

The Temple in Jerusalem has always been seen by Christians in later centuries as a symbol of the church of God. And that religious man of old, who wrote our psalm, had to make his way to the place of worship in a wicked and violent world, just as we do. He needed companions not just for friendship and fellowship, but for plain protection.

We make our way to the house of God, to the place of worship in a wicked and violent world. The same question faces us, as faced the psalmist. In his day it was 'What does Jerusalem stand for?' In our day it is 'What does the church of God need to stand for?'

One answer that he gave becomes clear when we look at the psalm as the NEB gives it. If you look at the AV you find, 'Jerusalem is builded as a city that is compact together,' which is the kind of point that a tourist guide might make. But the Hebrew words can bear a quite different meaning. The people who translated the Bible for our day were certain that this different meaning was the right one. 'Jerusalem that is built to be a city where people come together in unity,' and it goes on, 'To which the tribes resort, the tribes of the Lord, to give thanks to the Lord himself.'

It is not the city that is compact and unified; it is the city where *people* come together and are unified.

It was in fact for that purpose that David had established his capital and above all intended to build the Temple in Jerusalem. Here the twelve tribes, those little clans that differed from one another in temperament and in size and in much else, would find what brought them together and made them one. As they came up at the appropriate times of the year, at the atonement feast and the harvest festival and so on, to offer their thanksgiving and make their gifts in the worship of God's house, these so different and diverse people would find a unity in the deepest things of all.

Those deepest things were shown in the high priest entering the Holiest of Holies on the Day of Atonement, their need to render thanks to God for his goodness in bringing them into a land flowing with milk and honey, their need to recognize that life was not all getting and spending, but was made for larger and longer purposes, their need to realize freshly that God wanted them to care for one another and not just for themselves. When, different as they were, as different in terms shall we say of Scottish clans as the Campbells and Macdonalds, they came to Jerusalem, they would find that there was a unity which transcended their divisions, a oneness in their belonging to the Lord God who had so wonderfully led his people. 'Jerusalem that is built to be a city where people come together in unity.'

That is, of course, what the church of God is intended to be today. Sometimes the defence of separate denominations that is offered is that we are all so different we can hardly be expected to worship together. That would mean in Old Testament terms that there should not be any Jerusalem where people came together in unity. Let each tribe have its own meeting place for worship. Let everyone remain separate and never find their oneness in their common need of God's help, and their common rejoicing in what God has done.

It is not difficult to see why the psalmist put that first, that Jerusalem stood for what could make the whole family of tribes really one. His second answer is far more surprising. His second reason, why it was so specially good to go up to Jerusalem, reads:

> For in her are set the thrones of justice,
> the thrones of the house of David.   (NEB)

What an odd thought! 'I was glad when they said to me'–in Stow-on-the-Wold or Wigan or wherever–'let us go to London for a trip. For there are set theatres and the shops on Oxford Street, and picture galleries and sights to see like Buckingham Palace and Westminster Abbey.' But who ever heard a man say, 'I was glad when they said unto me, Let us go unto London, for there are set the Old Bailey and the Law Courts on the Strand'?

That is what the psalmist is saying. To the Hebrew the king was the fount of all justice. We have carried on that same conception in our own system of justice. We talk of the Queen's Bench and Queen's Counsel. Until very recently the circuit system was the reflection of the old idea many centuries ago of the king going on progress through his realm ministering justice. Criminal cases are still described as the Queen versus so-and-so, R (= Regina) versus Bloggs.

The Hebrew, moreover, thought more deeply about it than other peoples who might have the notion of the courts of justice being the king's courts. The Hebrew saw the duty of the king being to pass on the justice of God to the whole nation. The king's justice was not what pleased the king, but what pleased God, fair dealing between man and man, and the protection of the weak against the greed and malice of the strong.

With that in mind the verse means far more, for it is true and certain justice which does more than anything else for the family life of a nation, for their capacity to live together. Had the king's writ effectively run throughout the kingdom the psalmist would not have needed to wait for other people to want to go to Jerusalem. He could have gone alone when he was moved to do so. Real law and order mean freedom. Certain justice means an end to fear, fear of tyranny, fear of being victimized, fear of being pushed around at the whim of the brutal and the cruel.

The psalmist saw Jerusalem as symbolizing the place where there was certain and impartial justice given, that justice that God wanted, the sort of justice which stopped the savage and violent elements in men's hearts doing hurt to their brothers. Today we use 'law and order' almost as a dirty phrase, forgetting that 'thrones of justice' are our defence against the bully taking over. Justice is the defence of the ordinary man, the defence of the common life against those who would misuse power to bring about our ruin.

When at the close of the psalm the poet turns to prayer, prayer for the peace and prosperity of Jerusalem, there is a lovely phrase in the old version. It goes, 'For my brethren and companions' sake, I will say "Peace be within you".' It is as though the people he had travelled with, for whose company he had been glad because there was safety in numbers, had now become more than comforting and protective on the same journey. They had become true companions. The NEB goes, 'For the sake of these my brothers and my friends . . .'

The psalm begins with the man who wanted to go to Jerusalem, the 'I' of 'I was glad'. Other people were seen as useful to him. The fact that they also wanted to go made his journey possible in safety. It was rather like being glad there was a charter flight, the other people being bodies to fill the seats and keep the price down, and so make the journey possible. They did not matter as people. But with their journey to Jerusalem, and their common experience of their feet at last standing within the gates of the holy city, it had all changed. He cared about them now more than he cared about himself. And he prayed for Jerusalem to be all that it might be, a city of peace, and justice and of God's dwelling, more for the sake of others than for himself.

3   A Plea for a Fresh Start
Psalm 51

There is a very interesting paragraph in André Maurois' life of Alexander Fleming about a verse in this psalm. The great discoverer of penicillin only came upon the basic discovery by chance, his great powers of observation spotting a most unusual happening in the culture in one of his dishes. He was no expert in the science of classifying fungi. Eventually it was classified as a 'penicillium notatum'. Fleming learnt that it had originally been recognized by a Swedish chemist on a specimen of decayed hyssop. And immediately to the mind of Alexander Fleming, the Scot of Covenanting descent, nurtured on the Bible, and within the Bible very specially on the psalms, there rushed the words of this psalm: 'Purge me with hyssop and I shall be clean.' André Maurois adds, 'the first known reference to penicillin'.

That same book describes the rapturous reception that Fleming had across the world after the development of the great means of conquering so many diseases, and delivering so many from an early death. The honour was not just paid to him by his fellow scientists; streets were named in recognition of the greatness of his achievements, and ordinary folk showered on him their gifts–'A bootmaker, saved by penicillin, gave two pairs of shoes . . . a tailor two suits; a Spanish woman, miraculously cured, a sable stole; a grateful optician, a pair of gold-rimmed spectacles.' All this in Madrid, on one of his triumphant tours.

Why? Because for these people, or for those they loved, life had begun again when death had been closing in. When the dreaded crisis, say, in pneumonia had been mounting, this miraculous drug, developed from the mould that Fleming had observed to have such remarkable properties, had moved in to heal and to deliver.

It *is* striking, that curious modern link between that drug that has brought a new beginning in life for so many, and that ancient psalm which has as its theme the plea of an anguished heart for a new beginning. The psalm has as its theme not deliverance from physical disease and the threat of death, but deliverance from disease of the spirit, and from the things that kill a man's true humanity.

Now we may note the disturbing contrast between the man who offered deliverance from the grip of evil and the man who gave deliverance from disease and death. Fleming was feted; Jesus was crucified. The reflection forbids my making too glib and ready parallels here. Men are far more conscious of need when illness strikes than they are when moral rot sets in. A minister commented once that he observed at a dinner party that a man had only to reveal that he was a final year medical student for adjacent guests to be seeking informal consultations, but he, as a fully-trained and experienced minister, did not find the same thing happening in regard to his own alleged expertise. Deeper and more spiritual needs we try to hide, even from ourselves.

But there have been men who have been honest with themselves, and given us words which enable us to be honest with ourselves. Such a man was this psalmist. He wrote one of the great penitential psalms which has been on men's lips now for some two and a half thousand years and more. It is a poem of penitence so profound that though it was written some six or seven centuries before Christ's coming, it breathes the atmosphere of the New Testament rather than the Old. So strikingly true is this, that it seems that two verses were added later to it by another hand to continue to justify the system of blood sacrifices, away from which the noble spirit of this man had soared.

Noble spirit? *He* did not feel that. Where he began, at least, was in sheer personal failure. Or rather not quite there. In fact he began with God, God in his beauty and God in his holiness, or else he would not have cried:

> Have mercy on me, O God, in your goodness,
> in your great tenderness wipe away my faults.

Here indeed is the authentic New Testament note; it is the goodness of God that is heartbreaking, rather than the anger of a holy God that is terrifying, it is the tenderness of God, not his harshness, which brings about a deep sense of failure and a yearning for a new beginning. What the AV calls so beautifully 'the multitude of thy tender mercies', and the NEB 'the fullness of thy mercy' is both the ground of the psalmist's confidence that God will pardon, and the thought of God that evokes the sense of that desperate need.

And though, like all the psalms, this was used in the cultic worship of the Temple, and therefore was used to express the sense of corporate penitence, the need of a whole people for pardon, the thing which next strikes us about it–and makes it so remarkable coming as early as it does–is the sense of *individual* sin.

> For I am well aware of my faults,
> I have my sin continually in mind,
> having sinned against none other than you,
> having done what you regard as wrong.   (Jerusalem)

How freshly a new meaning comes in that last phrase, which is given in the AV as 'and have done this evil in your sight'. It is one thing to do an evil in front of God, it is another to see that a thing is evil because God regards it as wrong.

There are two comments which occur from looking at these verses as they come somewhat starkly in the Jerusalem Bible. One is to face a question: how can any man with a real sense of sin say 'having sinned against none other than you'? Is it not a plain fact that most of us only have any genuine sense of regret about wrong things that we have done if they have hurt some other person? The things that seem not to have had any effect on another, the internal sins, rather than the external ones, we do not take so seriously. (In fact, as has been said, most of us are often more distressed about our social lapses, our gaffes, the embarrassing things we have done, than about our moral lapses, but that is another issue.) Does it not suggest some blindness on the part of the psalmist when he says that it is only God against whom he has sinned? What about the other people affected by his behaviour, those harmed by his unkindness, or unhelped because of his selfishness? What about the people cut to the quick because of his sarcasm or cruel gossip? What about the people influenced by him to wrong ways–the kind of sin of which John Donne wrote:

> Wilt thou forgive that sin by which I have made
> others to sin, and made my sin their door?

But this question is really answered, at least in part, in the second comment. What the psalmist is doing is acknowledging his own sin, honestly recognizing a personal responsibility. For if it be true that he had caused others to sin, it was also true that they, or others, had influenced him in wrong ways. To quote other and well-known words of John Donne, 'No man is an island.' No, but every man is an individual, and must bear his responsibility. If you want to make a new beginning, get down to the roots, do not just pluck off the weed above ground.

What makes this cry of penitence of such lasting validity, so that men have been able to use it in every age, is that it sees sin as God sees it; it is offence against God, offence against the author of all goodness.

This admission is clearer when we move away from the confused utterance of the old translation, 'that thou might be justified when thou speakest, and be clear when thou judgest', to the NEB's

> so that thou mayest be proved right in thy charge
> and just in passing sentence,

or Jerusalem Bible's

> You are just when you pass sentence on me,
> blameless when you give judgment.

This psalm stresses the need for total honesty before God if a new beginning is to be made. When the psalmist cries, 'Wash me throughly from mine iniquity', the word used is one that reflects the way of washing dirty clothes then, as now in many less developed communities. The clothes were not just plunged in the stream, they were struck against the rocks, that the dirt which had permeated the fabric might be thoroughly knocked out. That is the cleansing the psalmist seeks, as deep-going, as thorough, and (if need be) as painful as that.

Our current tendency is to produce every ameliorating excuse for our way of behaviour and our character, possibly most of all that we are what we are because of our heredity. The psalmist does not forget that: for the often misunderstood lines:

> Behold, I was shapen in iniquity:
> and in sin did my mother conceive me,

do not, as they have often been understood as doing, imply a wrong notion of human sexuality, degrading it to something evil. They are a picture of original sin, if you like, and as Maclaren has said, ' "Original sin" is theological terminology for the same facts which science gathers together under the name or "heredity".' TEV gives these lines as:

> I have been evil from the time I was born;
> from the day of my birth I have been sinful.

That is, with life itself came an inheritance and part of that inheritance is that egotism which would centre life and everybody else on ourselves. Recognize that, but do not use it the wrong way, to explain and to excuse. Acknowledge the force of this in yourself and how much it has made you what you are if you want it to be dealt with.

> Take hyssop and sprinkle me, that I may be clean;
> wash me, that I may become whiter than snow;
> let me hear the sounds of joy and gladness,
> let the bones dance which thou hast broken.   (NEB)

What a curious, striking line is that last! Broken bones dancing. Another translation (Gélineau) is even more vivid:

> That the bones you have crushed may thrill.

What the psalmist is doing at this point, and elsewhere, is to recognize that there is something that has to be crushed and broken if a new beginning is to be made. The psalm ends with:

> My sacrifice, O God, is a broken spirit;
> a wounded heart, O God, thou wilt not despise.

Or even more compellingly in the Jerusalem version:

> My sacrifice is this broken spirit,
> you will not scorn this crushed and broken heart.

The 'something' is the arrogant egotism, the determination to have everything our own way, which is the heart of sin. It may not express itself necessarily in an obvious dominance. It may be very subtle, and all the more dangerous for that. There are egotists who never raise their voice, and say very little, but are determinedly planning all the time to have their own way. Nor is our egotism always a crude thing; sometimes it can hide itself in serving others, but the service is a way of ministering to our own self-importance. Some who would scorn place and position like to be surrounded with dependent people. The dirt of egotism is right into the fabric of the lives of most of us. 'Wash me *throughly* from mine iniquity.' There is something that has to be broken, a self-will that has to be crushed.

We may admire the amazing psychological and spiritual insight of this writer of long, long ago, but still wonder, 'Do we have to be so gloomy about human nature?' Are not in fact penitential psalms a thing of the past? To which there are two answers. One is: do we want new beginnings? Do we believe in new beginnings? Modern men who so readily dismiss the religious men of the past as gloomy with all their talk of sin are often in fact far, far more gloomy and pessimistic about human prospects than those whom they condemn. If all that can be said about man is that he is the creature of his heredity and environment you may have delivered him from beating his breast about his sins, but it is at the cost of depriving him of the chance of a new beginning. The psalmist may take human sin and egotism with a desperate seriousness, but he takes God's new beginning and the multitude of his tender mercies with a glorious hope.

The second answer is that the psalmist does not end in gloom at all. In fact his cry is 'Instil some joy and gladness in me' and his vision is of that which was broken, thrilling and dancing. 'Create a clean heart in me'—and the note to the word 'create' in the Jerusalem Bible is 'This verb always has God for its subject: it designates the act by which he brings something new and wonderful into being.' For what was poor and soiled he gives that which is new; for that which was unfaithful he gives that which is loyal; for that which was broken he gives that which can dance. Our religion is not one of penitential gloom, but one which takes our human condition seriously, and calls on us to face it honestly –and so facing it, put our trust in a God who can make a new thing, create a clean heart and put a fresh spirit within us.